Let's Get Cooking

MUFFINS
AND OTHER BAKES

Over **100** fantastic bakes

igloobooks

igloobooks

Published in 2017
by Igloo Books Ltd
Cottage Farm
Sywell
NN6 0BJ
www.igloobooks.com

Designed by Nicholas Gage
Edited by Bobby Newlyn-Jones

Food photography and recipe development
© Stockfood, The Food Media Agency
Additional imagery © iStock / Getty Images
Cover images: © iStock / Getty Images

LEO002 0417
2 4 6 8 10 9 7 5 3 1
ISBN 978-1-78670-918-9

Printed and manufactured in China

Contents

Muffins

Poppy Seed and Apricot Jam Muffins

1 large egg
120 ml / 4 fl. oz / ½ cup sunflower oil
120 ml / 4 fl. oz / ½ cup milk
375 g / 12 ½ oz / 2 ½ cups self-raising flour, sifted
1 tsp baking powder
200 g / 7 oz / ¾ cup caster (superfine) sugar
200 g / 7 oz / ⅔ cup apricot jam (jelly)
2 tbsp poppy seeds

1. Preheat the oven to 180°C (160°C fan) / 350F / gas 4 and oil 12 silicone muffin cases.
2. Beat the egg in a jug with the oil and milk.
3. Mix the flour, baking powder and sugar in a bowl.
4. Pour in the egg mixture and stir just enough to combine.
5. Divide half the mixture between the cases and top each one with a big spoonful of apricot jam.
6. Spoon the rest of the muffin mixture on top then sprinkle with poppy seeds.
7. Transfer the muffins to the oven and bake for 20–25 minutes.
8. Test with a wooden toothpick; if it comes out clean, the muffins are done.
9. Transfer the muffins to a wire rack and leave to cool completely.

MAKES: **24** | PREP TIME: **25 MINS** | COOKING TIME: **15-20 MINS**

Chocolate and Orange Mini Muffins

1 large egg
120 ml / 4 fl. oz / ½ cup sunflower oil
120 ml / 4 fl. oz / ½ cup milk
1 orange, juice and zest
375 g / 12 ½ oz / 2 ½ cups self-raising flour, sifted
1 tsp baking powder
2 tbsp cocoa powder
75 g / 2 ½ oz / ½ cup chocolate chips
75 g / 2 ½ oz / ½ cup candied orange peel, chopped
200 g / 7 oz / ¾ cup caster (superfine) sugar

1. Preheat the oven to 180°C (160°C fan) / 350F / gas 4 and line a 24-hole mini muffin tin with paper cases.
2. Beat the egg in a jug with the oil, milk and orange juice and zest until well mixed.
3. Mix the flour, baking powder, cocoa, chocolate chips, candied peel and sugar in a bowl.
4. Pour in the egg mixture and stir just enough to combine.
5. Divide the mixture between the paper cases and bake for 15–20 minutes.
6. Test with a wooden toothpick; if it comes out clean, the muffins are done.
7. Transfer the muffins to a wire rack and leave to cool completely.

Plain Muffins

1 large egg
120 ml / 4 fl. oz / ½ cup sunflower oil
120 ml / 4 fl. oz / ½ cup milk
375 g / 12 ½ oz / 2 cups self-raising
   flour, sifted
1 tsp baking powder
200 g / 7 oz / cup caster (superfine) sugar

1. Preheat the oven to 180°C (160°C fan) / 350F / gas 4 and oil 12 silicone
   muffin cases.
2. Beat the egg in a jug with the oil and milk until well mixed.
3. Mix the flour, baking powder and sugar in a bowl.
4. Pour in the egg mixture and stir just enough to combine.
5. Divide the mixture between the cases and bake for 20–25 minutes.
6. Test with a wooden toothpick; if it comes out clean, the muffins are done.
7. Transfer the muffins to a wire rack and leave to cool completely.

Raisin and Oat Muffins

1 large egg
120 ml / 4 fl. oz / ½ cup sunflower oil
120 ml / 4 fl. oz / ½ cup oat milk
300 g / 10 ½ oz / 2 cups self-raising
   flour, sifted
75 g / 2 ½ oz / ½ cup jumbo porridge oats
1 tsp baking powder
200 g / 7 oz / ¾ cup caster (superfine)
   sugar
75 g / 2 ½ oz / ½ cup raisins

1. Preheat the oven to 180°C (160° fan) / 350F / gas 4 and oil a 12-hole
   silicone muffin tin.
2. Beat the egg in a jug with the oil and milk until well mixed.
3. Mix the flour with two thirds of the oats and the baking powder, sugar and
   raisins. Pour in the egg mixture and stir just enough to combine.
4. Spoon the mixture into the moulds and sprinkle with the remaining oats, then
   bake in the oven for 20 minutes. Test with a toothpick; if it comes out clean,
   the muffins are done. If not, return to the oven for 5 minutes and test again.
5. Turn the muffins out onto a wire rack and leave to cool before serving.

MAKES: 24 | PREP TIME: 15 MINS | COOKING TIME: 10-15 MINS

Olive and Rosemary Mini Muffins

2 large eggs
120 ml / 4 fl. oz / ½ cup sunflower oil
180 ml / 6 fl. oz / ⅔ cup Greek yogurt
2 tbsp Parmesan, finely grated
225 g / 8 oz / 1 ½ cup plain (all-purpose) flour
2 tsp baking powder
½ tsp bicarbonate of (baking) soda
½ tsp salt
75 g / 2 ½ oz / ½ cup black olives, stoned and chopped
2 tbsp fresh rosemary, chopped

1. Preheat the oven to 180°C (160°C fan) / 350F / gas 4 and line a 24-hole mini muffin tin with paper cases.
2. Beat the egg in a jug with the oil, yogurt and cheese until well mixed.
3. Mix the flour, raising agents, salt, olives and rosemary in a bowl, then pour in the egg mixture and stir just enough to combine.
4. Divide the mixture between the paper cases, then bake in the oven for 10–15 minutes.
5. Test with a wooden toothpick; if it comes out clean, the muffins are done.
6. Serve warm.

Rose Petal Mini Muffins

1 large egg
120 ml / 4 fl. oz / ½ cup sunflower oil
120 ml / 4 fl. oz / ½ cup milk
1 tbsp rose water
375 g / 12 ½ oz / 2 ½ cups self-raising
   flour, sifted
1 tsp baking powder
200 g / 7 oz / ¾ cup caster (superfine)
   sugar

55 g / 2 oz / ½ cup ground almonds
2 tbsp crystallised rose petals
icing (confectioner's) sugar to dust

TO DECORATE
225 g / 8 oz / 2 ¼ cups icing
   (confectioner's) sugar
2–4 tsp rose water
crystallised rose petals

1. Preheat the oven to 180°C (160°C fan) / 350F / gas 4 and oil a 24-hole
   silicone mini muffin mould.
2. Beat the egg in a jug with the oil, milk and rose water until well mixed.
3. Mix the flour, baking powder, sugar, ground almonds and rose petals in
   a bowl, then pour in the egg mixture and stir just enough to combine.
4. Divide the mixture between the moulds and bake in the oven for
   15–20 minutes. Test with a wooden toothpick; if it comes out clean,
   the cakes are done.
5. Transfer the cakes to a wire rack and leave to cool before dusting with
   icing sugar.
6. To decorate, sieve the icing sugar into a bowl and add just enough rose
   water to make a thick icing.
7. Spoon the icing over the muffins and decorate with crystallised rose petals.

MAKES: 12 | PREP TIME: 25 MINS | COOKING TIME: 20-25 MINS

Wholemeal Chocolate Muffins

1 large egg
120 ml / 4 fl. oz / ½ cup sunflower oil
120 ml / 4 fl. oz / ½ cup milk
200 g / 7 oz / 1 ⅓ cups self-raising flour, sifted
175 g / 6 oz / 1 ¼ cups stoneground wholemeal flour
2 tbsp cocoa powder
2 tsp baking powder
200 g / 7 oz / ¾ cup caster (superfine) sugar
150 g / 5 ½ oz dark chocolate (minimum 60% cocoa solids), grated

TO DECORATE
dark chocolate sauce
1 tsp desiccated coconut

1. Preheat the oven to 180°C (160°C fan) / 350F / gas 4 and line a 12-hole muffin tin with paper cases.
2. Beat the egg in a jug with the oil and milk until well mixed.
3. Mix the flour, cocoa, baking powder, sugar and chocolate in a bowl.
4. Pour in the egg mixture and stir just enough to combine.
5. Divide the mixture between the paper cases and bake for 20–25 minutes.
6. Test with a wooden toothpick; if it comes out clean, the cakes are done.
7. Transfer the muffins to a wire rack and leave to cool completely.
8. Drizzle the dark chocolate sauce over each muffin and sprinkle with the desiccated coconut.

MAKES: 24 | PREP TIME: 25 MINS | COOKING TIME: 15-20 MINS

Pecan Mini Muffins

1 large egg

120 ml / 4 fl. oz / ½ cup sunflower oil

120 ml / 4 fl. oz / ½ cup milk

1 tsp vanilla extract

375 g / 12 ½ oz / 2 ½ cups self-raising flour, sifted

1 tsp baking powder

200 g / 7 oz / 1 ¼ cups soft brown sugar

55 g / 2 oz / ½ cup ground almonds

75 g / 2 ½ oz / ⅔ cup pecan nuts, chopped

1. Preheat the oven to 180°C (160°C fan) / 350F / gas 4 and oil a 24-hole silicone mini muffin mould.

2. Beat the egg in a jug with the oil, milk and vanilla extract until well mixed.

3. Mix the flour, baking powder, sugar, ground almonds and pecan nuts in a bowl, then pour in the egg mixture and stir just enough to combine.

4. Divide the mixture between the moulds and bake in the oven for 15–20 minutes.

5. Test with a wooden toothpick; if it comes out clean, the muffins are done.

6. Transfer the muffins to a wire rack and leave to cool completely.

Chocolate and Almond Muffins

1 large egg
125 ml / 4 ½ fl. oz / ½ cup almond oil
125 ml / 4 ½ fl. oz / ½ cup milk
1 tsp almond extract
250 g / 9 oz / 1 ⅔ cups self-raising flour, sifted
100 g / 3 ½ oz / 1 cup ground almonds
50 g / 1 ¾ oz / ½ cup unsweetened cocoa powder, sifted
1 tsp baking powder
200 g / 7 oz / ¾ cup caster (superfine) sugar
icing (confectioner's) sugar, for dusting

1. Preheat the oven to 180°C (160° fan) / 350F / gas 4 and line a 12-hole cupcake tin with paper cases.
2. Beat the egg in a jug with the oil, milk and almond extract until well mixed.
3. Mix the flour, ground almonds, cocoa, baking powder and sugar in a bowl, then pour in the egg mixture and stir just enough to combine.
4. Divide the mixture between the cases, then bake in the oven for 20 minutes. Test with a wooden toothpick; if it comes out clean, the muffins are done. If not, return to the oven for 5 minutes and test again.
5. Transfer to a wire rack and leave to cool before serving, dusted with icing sugar.

Fig and Honey Muffins

1 large egg
120 ml / 4 fl. oz / ½ cup sunflower oil
120 ml / 4 fl. oz / ½ cup milk
100 g / 3 ½ oz / ⅓ cup runny honey
375 g / 12 ½ oz / 2 ½ cups self-raising flour, sifted
1 tsp baking powder
100 g / 3 ½ oz / ½ cup caster (superfine) sugar
4 fresh figs, chopped

1. Preheat the oven to 180°C (160°C fan) / 350F / gas 4 and line a 12-hole muffin tin with greaseproof paper.
2. Beat the egg in a jug with the oil, milk and honey until well mixed.
3. Mix the flour, baking powder, and sugar in a bowl.
4. Pour in the egg mixture and stir just enough to combine then fold in the figs.
5. Divide the mixture between the paper cases and bake for 20–25 minutes.
6. Test with a wooden toothpick; if it comes out clean, the muffins are done.
7. Transfer the muffins to a wire rack and leave to cool completely.

MAKES: 12 | PREP TIME: 15 MINS | COOKING TIME: 20-25 MINS

Pumpkin Muffins

1 large egg
120 ml / 4 fl. oz / ½ cup sunflower oil
120 ml / 4 fl. oz / ½ cup milk
150 g / 4 ½ oz / 1 cups pumpkin,
  finely grated
375 g / 12 ½ oz / 2 cups self-raising
  flour, sifted
1 tsp baking powder
200 g / 7 oz / cup caster
  (superfine) sugar

TO DECORATE
4 tbsp cream cheese
2 tbsp icing (confectioner's) sugar
3 tbsp pumpkin seeds

1. Preheat the oven to 180°C (160°C fan) / 350F / gas 4 and line a 12-hole muffin tin with paper cases.
2. Beat the egg in a jug with the oil, milk and grated pumpkin until well mixed.
3. Mix the flour, baking powder and sugar in a bowl.
4. Pour in the egg mixture and stir just enough to combine.
5. Divide the mixture between the cases and bake for 20–25 minutes.
6. Test with a wooden toothpick; if it comes out clean, the muffins are done.
7. Transfer the muffins to a wire rack and leave to cool completely.
8. Whip the cream cheese with the icing sugar and spread it on top of the muffins with a palette knife.
9. Sprinkle over the pumpkin seeds.

MAKES: **24** | PREP TIME: **25 MINS** | COOKING TIME: **15-20 MINS**

Blackcurrant Mini Muffins

1 large egg

120 ml / 4 fl. oz / ½ cup sunflower oil

60 ml / 2 fl. oz / ¼ cup milk

60 ml / 2 fl. oz / ¼ cup blackcurrant cordial

375 g / 12 ½ oz / 2 ½ cups self-raising flour, sifted

1 tsp baking powder

200 g / 7 oz / ¾ cup caster (superfine) sugar

200 g / 7 oz / 1 ⅓ cups blackcurrants

1. Preheat the oven to 180°C (160°C fan) / 350F / gas 4 and line a 24-hole mini muffin tin with paper cases.

2. Beat the egg in a jug with the oil, milk and cordial until well mixed.

3. Mix the flour, baking powder and sugar in a bowl.

4. Pour in the egg mixture and stir just enough to combine then fold in the blackcurrants.

5. Divide the mixture between the paper cases and bake for 15–20 minutes.

6. Test with a wooden toothpick; if it comes out clean, the muffins are done.

7. Transfer the muffins to a wire rack and leave to cool completely.

MAKES: 24 | **PREP TIME: 15 MINS** | **COOKING TIME: 10-15 MINS**

Parmesan and Pistachio Mini Muffins

2 large eggs
120 ml / 4 fl. oz / ½ cup sunflower oil
180 ml / 6 fl. oz / ¾ cup Greek yogurt
100 g / 3 ½ oz / 1 cup Parmesan, grated
225 g / 8 oz / 1 ½ cup plain
  (all-purpose) flour
2 tsp baking powder
½ tsp bicarbonate of (baking) soda
½ tsp salt
75 g / 2 ½ oz / ½ cup pistachio nuts

1. Preheat the oven to 180°C (160°C fan) / 350F / gas 4 and line a 24-hole mini muffin tin with paper cases.
2. Beat the egg in a jug with the oil, yogurt and cheese until well mixed.
3. Mix the flour, raising agents, salt and pistachios in a bowl, then pour in the egg mixture and stir just enough to combine.
4. Divide the mixture between the paper cases, then bake in the oven for 10–15 minutes.
5. Test with a wooden toothpick; if it comes out clean, the muffins are done.
6. Serve warm.

MAKES: 12 | PREP TIME: 15 MINS | COOKING TIME: 20-25 MINS

Crab, Chilli and Lime Muffins

2 large eggs
120 ml / 4 fl. oz / ½ cup sunflower oil
180 ml / 6 fl. oz / ¾ cup Greek yogurt
2 tbsp Parmesan, finely grated
150 g / 5 ½ oz / ¾ cup fresh crab meat
1 red chilli (chili), finely chopped
1 lime, zest finely grated
1 tbsp coriander (cilantro) leaves, chopped
225 g / 8 oz / 1 ½ cup plain (all-purpose) flour
2 tsp baking powder
½ tsp bicarbonate of (baking) soda
½ tsp salt

1. Preheat the oven to 180°C (160°C fan) / 350F / gas 4 and oil a 12-hole silicone muffin mould.
2. Beat the egg in a jug with the oil, yogurt, Parmesan, crab, chilli, lime and coriander until well mixed.
3. Mix the flour, raising agents and salt in a bowl, then pour in the egg mixture and stir just enough to combine.
4. Divide the mixture between the moulds, then bake in the oven for 20–25 minutes.
5. Test with a wooden toothpick; if it comes out clean, the muffins are done.

Chocolate Chip Muffins

1 large egg
120 ml / 4 fl. oz / ½ cup sunflower oil
120 ml / 4 fl. oz / ½ cup milk
375 g / 12 ½ oz / 2 ½ cups self-raising flour, sifted
1 tsp baking powder
200 g / 7 oz / ¾ cup caster (superfine) sugar
150 g / 5 ½ oz / 1 cup chocolate chips

1. Preheat the oven to 180°C (160°C fan) / 350F / gas 4 and line a 12-hole muffin tin with paper cases.
2. Beat the egg in a jug with the oil and milk until well mixed.
3. Mix the flour, baking powder, sugar and chocolate chips in a bowl.
4. Pour in the egg mixture and stir just enough to combine.
5. Divide the mixture between the paper cases and bake for 20–25 minutes.
6. Test with a wooden toothpick; if it comes out clean, the muffins are done.
7. Transfer the muffins to a wire rack and leave to cool completely.

Blackberry Mini Muffins

1 large egg
120 ml / 4 fl. oz / ½ cup sunflower oil
120 ml / 4 fl. oz / ½ cup milk
375 g / 12 ½ oz / 2 ½ cups self-raising flour, sifted
1 tsp baking powder
200 g / 7 oz / ¾ cup caster (superfine) sugar
200 g / 7 oz / 1 ⅓ cups blackberries

1. Preheat the oven to 180°C (160°C fan) / 350F / gas 4 and line a 24-hole mini muffin tin with paper cases.
2. Beat the egg in a jug with the oil and milk until well mixed.
3. Mix the flour, baking powder and sugar in a bowl.
4. Pour in the egg mixture and stir just enough to combine then fold in the blackberries.
5. Divide the mixture between the paper cases and bake for 15–20 minutes.
6. Test with a wooden toothpick; if it comes out clean, the muffins are done.
7. Transfer the muffins to a wire rack and leave to cool completely.

MAKES: 12 | PREP TIME: 25 MINS | COOKING TIME: 20-25 MINS

Fig and Orange Muffins

1 large egg

120 ml / 4 fl. oz / ½ cup sunflower oil

120 ml / 4 fl. oz / ½ cup milk

375 g / 12 ½ oz / 2 ½ cups self-raising flour, sifted

1 tsp baking powder

200 g / 7 oz / ¾ cup caster (superfine) sugar

1 orange, zest finely grated

4 fresh figs, chopped

1. Preheat the oven to 180°C (160°C fan) / 350F / gas 4 and line a 12-hole muffin tin with greaseproof paper.
2. Beat the egg in a jug with the oil and milk until well mixed.
3. Mix the flour, baking powder, sugar and orange zest in a bowl.
4. Pour in the egg mix and stir just enough to combine then fold in the figs.
5. Divide the mixture between the paper cases and bake for 20–25 minutes.
6. Test with a wooden toothpick; if it comes out clean, the muffins are done.
7. Transfer the muffins to a wire rack and leave to cool completely.

MAKES: 12 | PREP TIME: 15 MINS | COOKING TIME: 20-25 MINS

Ginger Muffins

1 large egg
120 ml / 4 fl. oz / ½ cup sunflower oil
120 ml / 4 fl. oz / ½ cup milk
4 pieces stem ginger in syrup, chopped
375 g / 12 ½ oz / 2 cups self-raising flour, sifted
1 tsp baking powder
1 tsp ground ginger
200 g / 7 oz / ¾ cup caster (superfine) sugar

1. Preheat the oven to 180°C (160°C fan) / 355F / gas 4 and oil a 12-hole silicone oval muffin mould.
2. Beat the egg in a jug with the oil, milk and stem ginger until well mixed.
3. Mix the flour, baking powder, ground ginger and sugar in a bowl.
4. Pour in the egg mixture and stir just enough to combine.
5. Divide the mixture between the moulds and bake for 20–25 minutes.
6. Test with a wooden toothpick; if it comes out clean, the muffins are done.
7. Transfer the muffins to a wire rack and leave to cool completely.

Mixed Spice Muffins

1 large egg
120 ml / 4 fl. oz / ½ cup sunflower oil
120 ml / 4 fl. oz / ½ cup milk
375 g / 12 ½ oz / 2 ½ cups self-raising
   flour, sifted
1 tsp baking powder
2 tsp mixed spice
200 g / 7 oz / ¾ cup caster
   (superfine) sugar

1. Preheat the oven to 180°C (160°C fan) / 350F / gas 4 and line a 12-hole muffin tin with paper cases.
2. Beat the egg in a jug with the oil and milk until well mixed.
3. Mix the flour, baking powder, mixed spice and sugar in a bowl.
4. Pour in the egg mixture and stir just enough to combine.
5. Divide the mixture between the cases and bake for 20–25 minutes.
6. Test with a wooden toothpick; if it comes out clean, the muffins are done.
7. Transfer the muffins to a wire rack and leave to cool completely.

Peanut Muffins

1 large egg
120 ml / 4 fl. oz / ½ cup sunflower oil
120 ml / 4 fl. oz / ½ cup milk
375 g / 12 ½ oz / 2 ½ cups self-raising
   flour, sifted
1 tsp baking powder
200 g / 7 oz / ¾ cup caster
   (superfine) sugar
150 g / 5 ½ oz / 1 cup peanuts

1. Preheat the oven to 180°C (160°C fan) / 350F / gas 4 and line a 12-hole muffin tin with paper cases.
2. Beat the egg in a jug with the oil and milk until well mixed.
3. Mix the flour, baking powder, sugar and peanuts in a bowl.
4. Pour in the egg mixture and stir just enough to combine.
5. Divide the mixture between the paper cases and bake for 20–25 minutes.
6. Test with a wooden toothpick; if it comes out clean, the muffins are done.
7. Transfer the muffins to a wire rack and leave to cool completely.

Cakes

MAKES: 12 | PREP TIME: 20 MINS | COOKING TIME: 15-20 MINS

Flower Cupcakes

110 g / 4 oz / ⅔ cup self-raising flour, sifted
110 g / 4 oz / ½ cup caster (superfine) sugar
110 g / 4 oz / ½ cup butter, softened
2 large eggs
1 tsp vanilla extract
110 g / 4 oz / ½ butter, softened
225 g / 8 oz / 2 ¼ cups icing (confectioner's) sugar
2 tbsp milk
a few drops of food dye
sugar flowers to decorate

1. Preheat the oven to 190°C (170°C fan) / 375F / gas 5 and line a 12-hole cupcake tin with paper cases.

2. Combine the flour, sugar, butter, eggs and vanilla extract in a bowl and whisk together until smooth.

3. Divide the mixture between the paper cases, then bake for 15–20 minutes.

4. Test with a wooden toothpick; if it comes out clean, the cakes are done.

5. Transfer the cakes to a wire rack and leave to cool.

6. To make the buttercream, beat the butter with a wooden spoon until light and fluffy then beat in the icing sugar a quarter at a time. Use a whisk to incorporate the milk then whisk until smooth.

7. Divide the buttercream into separate bowls and stir in the food colourings of your choice.

8. Spread the buttercream onto the cakes and decorate each one with a sugar flower.

SERVES: 10-12 | **PREP TIME: 10 MINS** | **COOKING TIME: 40-45 MINS**

Chocolate Ganache Gateau

FOR THE CAKE
110 g / 4 oz / ⅔ cup self-raising flour
28 g / 1 oz / ¼ cup unsweetened
  cocoa powder
1 tsp baking powder
110 g / 4 oz / ½ cup caster (superfine)
  sugar
110 g / 4 oz / ½ cup butter
2 large eggs

FOR THE GANACHE
300 ml / 10 ½ fl. oz / 1 ¼ cups double
  (heavy) cream
300 g / 10 ½ oz dark chocolate,
  chopped
75 g / 2 ½ oz / ⅓ cup butter, cubed

FOR THE WHITE CHOCOLATE CURLS
100 g / 3 ½ oz white chocolate

1. Preheat the oven to 180°C (160°C fan) / 350F / gas 4 and grease and line
   a 20 cm round spring-form cake tin.
2. Whisk together the cake ingredients with an electric whisk.
3. Scrape the mixture into the tin and bake for 30–35 minutes.
4. The cake is ready when a toothpick inserted comes out clean.
5. Transfer the cake to a wire rack to cool before slicing in half horizontally.
6. Bring the cream to simmering point then pour it over the chocolate and
   stir until smooth.
7. Blend in the butter with a stick blender.
8. Clean the cake tin and line with cling film. Put a cake layer in the tin and
   pour over half of the ganache.
9. Top with the second cake layer and pour the rest of the ganache on top.
   Level the surface and chill for 4 hours.
10. Melt the white chocolate in a microwave or bain-marie and spread it onto
    a clean chopping board or marble slab.
11. When it has set, but before it becomes brittle, use a wallpaper scraper
    to make it into curls.

Cranberry Sponges

175 g / 6 oz / 1 ¼ cups self-raising flour
2 tsp baking powder
175 g / 6 oz / ¾ cup caster
  (superfine) sugar
175 g / 6 oz / ¾ cup butter
3 eggs
200 g / 7 oz / 1 ⅓ cups cranberries

1. Preheat the oven to 180°C (160°C fan) / 350F / gas 4 and grease and
   6 individual cake tins.
2. Put the flour, baking powder, sugar, butter and eggs in a mixing bowl
   and whisk them together with an electric whisk for 4 minutes or until pale
   and well whipped.
3. Fold in the cranberries and divide the mixture between the tins.
4. Bake for 20–25 minutes. The cakes are ready when a toothpick inserted
   comes out clean.
5. Transfer the cakes to a wire rack to cool completely.

Mini Apricot
Loaf Cakes

110 g / 4 oz / ⅔ cup self-raising flour,
  sifted
110 g / 4 oz / ½ cup caster
  (superfine) sugar
110 g / 4 oz / ½ cup butter, softened
2 large eggs
1 tsp vanilla extract
75 g / 2 ½ oz / ⅓ cup dried
  apricots, chopped

1. Preheat the oven to 190°C (170°C fan) / 375F / gas 5 and oil a 12-hole
   silicone mini loaf cake mould.
2. Combine the flour, sugar, butter, eggs and vanilla in a bowl and whisk
   together for 2 minutes or until smooth. Fold in the chopped apricots.
3. Divide the mixture between the moulds, then transfer the mould to the
   oven and bake for 15–20 minutes.
4. Test with a wooden toothpick; if it comes out clean, the cakes are done.
5. Transfer the cakes to a wire rack and leave to cool completely.

SERVES: 8 | PREP TIME: 25 MINS | COOKING TIME: 30-35 MINS

Almond and Honey Cake

55 g / 2 oz / ⅓ cup self-raising flour, sifted

55 g / 2 oz / ½ cup ground almonds

55 g / 2 oz / ½ cup caster (superfine) sugar

110 g / 4 oz / ⅓ cup honey

110 g / 4 oz / ½ cup butter, softened

2 large eggs

1 tsp almond essence

FOR THE TOPPING

4 tbsp runny honey

60 g / 2 oz flaked (slivered) almonds

1. Preheat the oven to 190°C (170°C fan) / 375F / gas 5 and grease and line a 23 cm round cake tin.
2. Combine the flour, ground almonds, sugar, honey, butter, eggs and almond essence in a bowl and whisk together for 2 minutes or until smooth.
3. Scrape the mixture into the prepared tin and bake for 30–35 minutes.
4. Test with a wooden toothpick; if it comes out clean, the cake is done.
5. Mix the honey and almonds together and spoon it on top of the cake.
6. Return the cake to the oven for 5 minutes or until the honey melts into the cake and the almonds turn golden.
7. Transfer the cake to a wire rack to cool.

Almond Cakes

55 g / 2 oz / ⅓ cup self-raising flour,
  sifted
1 tsp baking powder
55 g / 2 oz / ½ cup ground almonds
110 g / 4 oz / ½ cup caster (superfine)
  sugar
110 g / 4 oz / ½ cup butter, softened
2 large eggs

1. Preheat the oven to 190°C (170°C fan) / 375 / gas 5 and oil a 6-hole silicone
   tartlet mould or 6 individual tartlet tins.
2. Combine all of the ingredients in a bowl and whisk together for 2 minutes
   or until smooth.
3. Divide between the tins and bake for 20–25 minutes.
4. Test with a wooden toothpick; if it comes out clean, the cakes are done.
5. Transfer the cakes to a wire rack to cool before serving.

Gluten-free Coconut Cake

225 g / 8 oz / 1 cup butter, softened
225 g / 8 oz / 1 cup caster
  (superfine) sugar
1 vanilla pod, seeds only
4 large eggs, beaten
225 g / 4 ½ oz / 1 ½ cups rice flour
1 tsp baking powder
100 g / 3 ½ oz / 1 cup desiccated
  coconut

1. Preheat the oven to 180°C (160°C fan) / 350F / gas 4 and grease and line
   a 23 cm round cake tin with greaseproof paper.
2. Cream the butter, sugar and vanilla seeds together until well whipped
   then gradually whisk in the eggs, beating well after each addition.
3. Fold in the flour and coconut then scrape the mixture into the tin.
4. Bake the cake for 45–55 minutes or until a skewer inserted in the centre
   comes out clean.

SERVES: **8** | PREP TIME: **10 MINS** | COOKING TIME: **45-50 MINS**

Chocolate and Almond Marble Loaf

100 g / 3 ½ oz / ⅔ cup self-raising flour
1 tsp baking powder
50 g / 1 ¾ oz / ½ cup ground almonds
150 g / 5 ½ oz / ⅔ cup caster (superfine) sugar
150 g / 5 ½ oz / ⅔ cup butter
3 large eggs
2 tbsp cocoa powder
4 tbsp flaked (slivered) almonds

1. Preheat the oven to 180°C (160°C fan) / 350F / gas 4 and line a loaf tin with greaseproof paper.
2. Sieve the flour and baking powder into a mixing bowl then add the ground almonds, sugar, butter and eggs and whisk with an electric whisk for 4 minutes or until pale and well whipped.
3. Divide the mixture into 2 bowls. Mix the cocoa powder with 2 tbsp hot water until smooth and stir it into one of the bowls.
4. Spoon the mixture into the tin, alternating between chocolate and plain, then draw a knife down the centre to marble.
5. Sprinkle with flaked almonds and bake for 45-50 minutes. The cake is ready when a toothpick inserted in the centre comes out clean.
6. Transfer the cake to a wire rack to cool completely.

Apple and Cinnamon Loaf Cake

300 g / 10 ½ oz / 2 cups self-raising flour
2 tsp ground cinnamon
2 tsp baking powder
250 g / 9 oz / 1 ½ cups light brown
   sugar
250 g / 9 oz / 1 ¼ cups butter, softened
5 large eggs
2 eating apples, cored and chopped

1. Preheat the oven to 170°C (150°C fan) / 340F / gas 3 and line a large loaf tin with non-stick baking paper.
2. Sieve the flour, cinnamon and baking powder into a mixing bowl and add the sugar, butter and eggs.
3. Beat the mixture with an electric whisk for 4 minutes or until smooth and well whipped.
4. Fold in the chopped apples and scrape the mixture into the loaf tin.
5. Bake for 55 minutes or until a skewer inserted comes out clean.
6. Transfer the cake to a wire rack and leave to cool completely.

Mini Berry Cupcakes

110 g / 4 oz / 1 cup self-raising
   flour, sifted
110 g / 4 oz / ½ cup caster
   (superfine) sugar
110 g / 4 oz / ½ cup butter, softened
2 large eggs
1 tsp vanilla extract
18 raspberries
18 blackberries

1. Preheat the oven to 190°C (170°C fan) / 375F / gas 5 and line a 36 hole cupcake tin with paper cases.
2. Combine the flour, sugar, butter, eggs and vanilla extract in a bowl and whisk together for 2 minutes or until smooth.
3. Divide the mixture between the paper cases and press a berry into the top of each one.
4. Transfer the tin to the oven and bake for 10–15 minutes.
5. Test with a wooden toothpick; if it comes out clean, the cakes are done.
6. Transfer the cakes to a wire rack and leave to cool completely.

SERVES: 8-10 | **PREP TIME: 10 MINS** | **COOKING TIME: 35-40 MINS**

Cherry and Honey Cake

300 g / 10 ½ oz / 2 cups self-raising
  flour
2 tsp baking powder
125 g / 4 ½ oz / ½ cup caster
  (superfine) sugar
125 g / 4 ½ oz / ⅓ cup runny honey
250 g / 9 oz / 1 ¼ cup butter, softened
5 large eggs
150 g / 5 oz / 1 cup cherries, halved
  and stoned

1. Preheat the oven to 170°C (150°C
   fan) / 340F / gas 3 and line a
   23 cm round spring form cake
   tin with greaseproof paper.
2. Sieve the flour and baking powder
   into a mixing bowl and add the
   sugar, honey, butter and eggs.
3. Beat the mixture with an electric
   whisk for 4 minutes or until smooth
   and well whipped.
4. Arrange the cherries in the
   prepared cake tin then spoon
   the cake mixture on top.
5. Bake for 35–40 minutes or until
   a skewer inserted in the centre
   comes out clean.
6. Transfer the cake to a wire rack
   and leave to cool completely.

SERVES: 8-10 | PREP TIME: 5 MINS | COOKING TIME: 45-55 MINS

Coconut Cake with Redcurrant Compote

225 g / 8 oz / 1 cup butter, softened

225 g / 8 oz / 1 cup caster (superfine) sugar

4 large eggs, beaten

225 g / 4 ½ oz / 1 ½ cups self-raising flour

100 g / 3 ½ oz / 1 cup desiccated coconut

FOR THE COMPOTE

100 g / 3 ½ oz / ⅔ cup redcurrants

4 tbsp caster (superfine) sugar

1. Preheat the oven to 180°C (160°C fan) / 350F / gas 4 and grease and line a 23 cm round cake tin with greaseproof paper.
2. Cream the butter and sugar together then gradually whisk in the eggs, beating well after each addition.
3. Fold in the flour and coconut then scrape the mixture into the tin.
4. Bake the cake for 45–55 minutes or until a skewer inserted in the centre comes out clean.
5. Meanwhile, put the redcurrants in a small saucepan with the sugar. Cover and cook gently for 5 minutes then remove the lid, give it a stir and cook for a few more minutes until the redcurrants start to burst and the juices thicken.
6. Leave the cake to cool for 20 minutes before serving warm with the compote spooned over the top.

Apple and Poppy Seed Cake

300 g / 10 ½ oz / 2 cups self-raising flour
2 tsp baking powder
250 g / 9 oz / 1 ½ cups dark brown sugar
250 g / 9 oz / 1 ¼ cups butter, softened
5 large eggs
2 tbsp poppy seeds
1 tbsp caster (superfine) sugar
3 eating apples, cored and sliced

1. Preheat the oven to 170°C (150°C fan) / 340F / gas 3 and butter a round baking dish.
2. Sieve the flour and baking powder into a mixing bowl and add the brown sugar, butter, eggs and half the poppy seeds.
3. Beat the mixture with an electric whisk for 4 minutes or until smooth and well whipped.
4. Sprinkle the rest of the poppy seeds and the caster sugar over the base of the baking dish and arrange the apple slices on top.
5. Spoon the cake mixture on top of the apple and bake for 45 minutes or until a skewer inserted comes out clean.
6. Leave the cake to cool for 20 minutes before turning out onto a serving plate.

Chocolate and Mandarin Cake

300 g / 10 ½ oz / 2 cups self-raising flour
28 g / 1 oz / ¼ cup unsweetened
  cocoa powder
2 tsp baking powder
250 g / 9 oz / 1 ¼ cup caster
  (superfine) sugar
250 g / 9 oz / 1 ¼ cup butter, softened
5 large eggs
1 can mandarin segments in syrup,
  drained

1. Preheat the oven to 170°C (150°C fan) / 340F / gas 3 and butter a
   23 cm round cake tin.
2. Sieve the flour, cocoa and baking powder into a mixing bowl and add sugar,
   butter and eggs.
3. Beat the mixture with an electric whisk for 4 minutes until smooth.
4. Arrange the mandarin segments in the bottom of the tin and spoon the
   cake mixture on top.
5. Bake for 35 minutes or until a skewer inserted comes out clean.
6. Leave the cake to cool for 20 minutes before turning out onto a serving plate.

Vanilla Sponge Rings

110 g / 4 oz butter
55 g / 2 oz / ⅓ cup plain (all-purpose)
  flour
55 g / 2 oz / ½ cup ground almonds
110 g / 4 oz / 1 cup icing (confectioner's)
  sugar
3 large egg whites
1 vanilla pod, seeds only

1. Preheat the oven to 170°C (150°C fan) / 340F / gas 3 and oil and flour
   12 mini ring moulds.
2. Heat the butter until it foams and starts to smell nutty then leave to cool.
3. Combine the flour, ground almonds and icing sugar in a bowl and whisk in
   the egg whites and vanilla seeds.
4. Pour the cooled butter through a sieve into the bowl and whisk into the
   mixture until evenly mixed.
5. Spoon the mixture into the moulds, then transfer the tin to the oven and
   bake for 10–15 minutes.
6. Test with a wooden toothpick; if it comes out clean, the cakes are done.
7. Transfer the cakes to a wire rack to cool for 5 minutes before serving.

MAKES: **12** | PREP TIME: **1 HOUR** | COOKING TIME: **15-20 MINS**

Peach Cupcakes

1 can peach slices, drained, syrup reserved

110 g / 4 oz / ⅔ cup self-raising flour, sifted

110 g / 4 oz / ½ cup caster (superfine) sugar

110 g / 4 oz / ½ cup butter, softened

2 large eggs

300 ml / 10 ½ fl. oz / 1 ¼ cups double (heavy) cream

1. Preheat the oven to 190°C (170°C fan) / 375F / gas 5 and line a 12-hole cupcake tin with paper cases.

2. Reserve 12 of the peach slices and finely chop the rest. Combine the flour, sugar, butter, eggs and chopped peaches in a bowl and whisk together for 2 minutes or until smooth.

3. Divide the mixture between the paper cases, then transfer the tin to the oven and bake for 15–20 minutes.

4. Test with a wooden toothpick; if it comes out clean, the cakes are done.

5. Transfer the cakes to a wire rack and leave to cool completely.

6. Whip the cream until thick then fill a piping bag fitted with a large star nozzle and pipe a rosette on top of each cake.

7. Lay a slice of peach next to the cream and drizzle a little of the reserved peach syrup on top.

Poppy Seed Cake

225 g / 8 oz / 1 ½ cups self-raising flour
100 g / 3 ½ oz / ½ cup butter, cubed
100 g / 3 ½ oz / ½ cup caster (superfine) sugar
2 tbsp poppy seeds
1 large egg
75 ml / 3 ½ fl. oz / ⅓ cup whole milk

1. Preheat the oven to 180°C (160°C fan) / 350F / gas 4 and line a 23 cm round cake tin with non-stick baking paper.
2. Sieve the flour into a mixing bowl and rub in the butter until it resembles fine breadcrumbs then stir in the sugar and poppy seeds.
3. Lightly beat the egg with the milk and stir it into the dry ingredients until just combined.
4. Scrape the mixture into the tin and bake for 55 minutes or until a skewer inserted comes out clean.
5. Transfer the cake to a wire rack and leave to cool completely.
6. Sprinkle with icing sugar.

Banana and Walnut Loaf Cake

3 very ripe bananas
110 g / 4 oz / ½ cup soft light brown sugar
2 large eggs
120 ml / 4 fl. oz / ½ cup sunflower oil
225 g / 8 oz / 1 ½ cup plain (all-purpose) flour
1 tsp bicarbonate of (baking) soda
75 g / 2 ½ oz / ⅔ cup walnuts, chopped

1. Preheat the oven to 170°C (150°C fan) / 340F / gas 3 and line a long thin loaf tin with non-stick baking paper.
2. Mash the bananas roughly with a fork then whisk in the sugar, eggs and oil.
3. Sieve the flour and bicarbonate of soda into the bowl and add the chopped walnuts. Stir just enough to evenly mix all the ingredients together.
4. Scrape the mixture into the loaf tin and bake for 55 minutes or until a skewer inserted comes out clean.
5. Transfer the cake to a wire rack and leave to cool completely.

SERVES: **8** | PREP TIME: **15 MINS** | COOKING TIME: **55 MINS**

Light Fruit Cake

225 g / 8 oz / 1 ½ cups self-raising flour
100 g / 3 ½ oz / ½ cup butter, cubed
100 g / 3 ½ oz / ½ cup caster (superfine) sugar
100 g / 3 ½ oz / ⅔ cup mixed dried fruit
8 glacé cherries, quartered
1 tsp grated lemon zest
1 large egg
75 ml / 2 ½ fl. oz / 1 ⅓ cups whole milk

1. Preheat the oven to 180°C (160°C fan) / 350F / gas 4 and line a loaf tin with non-stick baking paper.
2. Sieve the flour into a mixing bowl and rub in the butter until it resembles fine breadcrumbs then stir in the sugar, dried fruit, cherries and lemon zest.
3. Lightly beat the egg with the milk and stir it into the dry ingredients until just combined.
4. Scrape the mixture into the loaf tin and bake for 55 minutes or until a skewer inserted comes out clean.
5. Transfer the cake to a wire rack and leave to cool completely.

SERVES: 8 | PREP TIME: 15 MINS | COOKING TIME: 35 MINS

Pineapple Upside-down Cake

300 g / 10 ½ oz / 2 cups self-raising flour
2 tsp baking powder
250 g / 9 oz / 1 ¼ cups caster (superfine) sugar
250 g / 9 oz / 1 ¼ cups butter, softened
5 large eggs
4 tbsp raspberry jam (jelly)
4 canned pineapple rings, drained

1. Preheat the oven to 170°C (150°C fan) / 340F / gas 3 and butter a 23 cm round cake tin.
2. Sieve the flour and baking powder into a mixing bowl and add sugar, butter and eggs.
3. Beat the mixture with an electric whisk for 4 minutes or until smooth.
4. Spread the jam over the base of the cake tin and arrange the pineapple rings on top.
5. Spoon in the cake mixture and bake for 35 minutes or until a skewer inserted comes out clean.
6. Leave the cake to cool for 20 minutes before turning out onto a serving plate.

SERVES: 8-10 | PREP TIME: 15 MINS | COOKING TIME: 40-50 MINS

Chocolate Truffle Loaf Cake

600 g / 1 lb 5 oz / 2 ¾ cups
  cream cheese
150 ml / 5 fl. oz / ⅔ cup soured cream
175g / 6 oz / ¾ cup caster
  (superfine) sugar
2 large eggs
1 egg yolk
2 tbsp plain (all-purpose) flour
2 tbsp cocoa powder, plus extra
  for dusting
200 g / 7 oz dark chocolate (minimum
  60 % cocoa solids), melted

1. Preheat the oven to 180°C (160°C fan) / 350F / gas 4 and grease and line a large loaf tin with greaseproof paper.
2. Put all of the ingredients in a bowl and whisk together until smooth.
3. Scrape the mixture into the loaf tin and level the top with a palette knife.
4. Put the loaf tin in a large roasting tin and pour around enough boiling water to come half way up the side of the loaf tin.
5. Bake the cake for 40–50 minutes or until the centre is only just set.
6. Leave to cool completely in the tin then refrigerate for 2 hours before turning out and dusting with cocoa.

Gluten and Dairy-free Banana Loaf Cake

3 very ripe bananas
110 g / 4 oz / ½ cup caster (superfine) sugar
2 large eggs
120 ml / 4 fl. oz / ½ cup sunflower oil
175 g / 6 oz / 1 ¼ cups rice flour
50 g / 1 ¾ oz / ⅓ cup ground almonds
2 tsp baking powder

1. Preheat the oven to 170°C (150°C fan) / 340F / gas 3 and line a medium loaf tin with non-stick baking paper.
2. Mash the bananas well with a fork then whisk in the sugar, eggs and oil.
3. Sieve the rice flour and baking powder into the bowl and add the ground almonds. Stir just enough to evenly mix all the ingredients together.
4. Scrape the mixture into the loaf tin and bake for 55 minutes or until a skewer inserted comes out clean.
5. Transfer the cake to a wire rack and leave to cool completely.

Apricot Cupcakes

110 g / 4 oz / ⅔ cup self-raising flour, sifted
110 g / 4 oz / ½ cup caster (superfine) sugar
110 g / 4 oz / ½ cup butter, softened
2 large eggs
1 tsp vanilla extract
12 canned apricot halves, drained

1. Preheat the oven to 190°C (170°C fan) / 375F / gas 5 and line a 12-hole cupcake tin with paper cases.
2. Combine the flour, sugar, butter, eggs and vanilla extract in a bowl and whisk together for 2 minutes or until smooth.
3. Divide the mixture between the paper cases and press an apricot half into each one.
4. Transfer the tin to the oven and bake for 15–20 minutes.
5. Test with a wooden toothpick; if it comes out clean, the cakes are done.
6. Transfer the cakes to a wire rack and leave to cool completely.

SERVES: **8** | PREP TIME: **15 MINS** | COOKING TIME: **55 MINS**

Peach Cake with Lemon Thyme Sugar

225 g / 8 oz / 1 ½ cups self-raising flour
100 g / 3 ½ oz / ½ cup butter, cubed
100 g / 3 ½ oz / ½ cup caster (superfine) sugar
1 large egg
75 ml / 2 ½ fl. oz / ⅓ cup whole milk
4 peaches, halved and stoned

FOR THE LEMON THYME SUGAR
1 tbsp lemon thyme leaves
60 g / 2 oz / ¼ cup caster (superfine) sugar

1. Preheat the oven to 180°C (160°C fan) / 350F / gas 4 and butter a round baking dish.
2. First make the lemon thyme sugar. Bruise the thyme leaves with a pestle and mortar then add half the sugar and pound again. Stir in the rest of the sugar and set aside.
3. Sieve the flour into a mixing bowl and rub in the butter until it resembles fine breadcrumbs then stir in the sugar.
4. Lightly beat the egg with the milk and stir it into the dry ingredients until just combined.
5. Scrape the mixture into the baking dish and level the surface then press in the peach halves, cut side up.
6. Bake the cake for 55 minutes or until a skewer inserted comes out clean.
7. Transfer the cake to a wire rack and sprinkle with the lemon thyme sugar then leave to cool completely.

MAKES: 6 | PREP TIME: 10 MINS | COOKING TIME: 30 MINS

Strawberry Meringue Cakes

110 g / 4 oz / ⅔ cup self-raising
  flour, sifted
1 tsp baking powder
110 g / 4 oz / ½ cup caster
  (superfine) sugar
110 g / 4 oz / ½ cup butter, softened
2 large eggs
6 tbsp strawberry jam (jelly)
400 g / 14 oz strawberries, sliced
2 tbsp toasted flaked (slivered) almonds
2 tbsp pistachio nuts, chopped

FOR THE MERINGUE
4 large egg whites
110 g / 4 oz / ½ cup caster
  (superfine) sugar

1. Preheat the oven to 190°C (170°C fan) / 375F / gas 5 and oil a 6-hole silicone tartlet mould or 6 tartlet tins.
2. Combine the flour, baking powder, sugar, butter and eggs in a bowl and whisk together for 2 minutes.
3. Divide between the tins and bake for 20–25 minutes. Test with a wooden toothpick; if it comes out clean, the cakes are done.
4. Turn the cakes out onto a large baking tray and spread the tops with strawberry jam.
5. Whisk the egg whites until stiff, then gradually whisk in half the sugar until the mixture is shiny.
6. Fold in the remaining sugar then spoon the meringue on top of the cakes, allowing it to ooze down the sides.
7. Return the cakes to the oven and cook for 10 minutes.
8. Leave the cakes to cool before topping them with sliced strawberries and nuts.

SERVES: **8** | PREP TIME: **10 MINS** | COOKING TIME: **45-50 MINS**

Chocolate and Almond Loaf Cake

100 g / 3 ½ oz / ⅔ cup self-raising flour
1 tsp baking powder
2 tbsp cocoa powder
50 g / 1 ¾ oz / ½ cup ground almonds
150 g / 5 ½ oz / ⅔ cup caster (superfine) sugar
150 g / 5 ½ oz / ⅔ cup butter
3 large eggs
100 g / 3 ½ oz dark chocolate (minimum 60 % cocoa solids), chopped
100 g / 3 ½ oz / ⅔ cup blanched almonds

1. Preheat the oven to 180°C (160°C fan) / 350F / gas 4 and butter a terrine dish.
2. Sieve the flour, baking powder and cocoa into a mixing bowl then add the ground almonds, sugar, butter and eggs and whisk with an electric whisk for 4 minutes or until pale and well whipped.
3. Fold in the chocolate and almonds and spoon into the terrine, then bake for 45–50 minutes.
4. The cake is ready when a toothpick inserted in the centre comes out clean.
5. Transfer the cake to a wire rack to cool completely.

SERVES: 8 | PREP TIME: 15 MINS | COOKING TIME: 55 MINS

Plum and Honey Loaf Cake

225 g / 8 oz / 1 ½ cups self-raising flour

100 g / 3 ½ oz / ½ cup butter, cubed

85 g / 3 oz / ⅓ cup caster (superfine) sugar

4 plums, stoned and chopped

1 large egg

75 ml / 2 ½ fl. oz / ⅓ cup whole milk

3 tbsp runny honey

1. Preheat the oven to 180°C (160°C fan) / 350F / gas 4 and line a loaf tin with non-stick baking paper.
2. Sieve the flour into a mixing bowl and rub in the butter until it resembles fine breadcrumbs, then stir in the sugar and plums.
3. Lightly beat the egg with the milk and honey then stir it into the dry ingredients until just combined.
4. Scrape the mixture into the loaf tin and bake for 55 minutes or until a skewer inserted comes out clean.
5. Transfer the cake to a wire rack and leave to cool completely.

MAKES: **12** | PREP TIME: **20 MINS** | COOKING TIME: **15-20 MINS**

Chocolate and Pistachio Cupcakes

110 g / 4 oz / ⅔ cup self-raising flour, sifted
28 g / 1 oz cocoa powder
110 g / 4 oz / ½ cup caster (superfine) sugar
110 g / 4 oz / ½ cup butter, softened
2 large eggs
1 tsp almond essence

TO DECORATE
225 g / 8 oz / 2 ¼ cups icing (confectioner's) sugar
½ tsp almond essence
3 tbsp pistachio nuts, chopped

1. Preheat the oven to 190°C (170°C fan) / 375F / gas 5 and line a 12-hole cupcake tin with paper cases.
2. Combine the flour, sugar, butter, eggs and vanilla extract in a bowl and whisk together for 2 minutes or until smooth.
3. Divide the mixture between the paper cases, then transfer the tin to the oven and bake for 15–20 minutes.
4. Test with a wooden toothpick; if it comes out clean, the cakes are done.
5. Transfer the cakes to a wire rack and leave to cool completely before peeling off the papers.
6. To make the icing, sieve the icing sugar into a bowl and add the almond essence. Stir in enough hot water, drop by drop, to form a spreadable icing and spoon it over the cakes.
7. Sprinkle with chopped pistachios and leave the icing to set.

Clementine Upside-down Cake

300 g / 10 ½ oz / 2 cups self-raising flour
2 tsp baking powder
250 g / 9 oz / 1 ¼ cups caster
   (superfine) sugar
250 g / 9 oz / 1 ¼ cups butter, softened
5 large eggs
4 tbsp golden syrup
4 clementines, thinly sliced

1. Preheat the oven to 170°C (150°C fan) / 340F / gas 3 and butter a 23 cm round cake tin.
2. Sieve the flour and baking powder into a mixing bowl and add sugar, butter and eggs.
3. Beat the mixture with an electric whisk for 4 minutes or until smooth and well whipped.
4. Spread the golden syrup over the base of the cake tin and arrange the clementine slices on top and up the sides of the tin.
5. Spoon in the cake mixture and bake for 35 minutes or until a skewer inserted in the centre comes out clean.
6. Leave the cake to cool for 20 minutes before turning out onto a serving plate.

Chocolate Loaf Cake

225 g / 8 oz / 1 cup butter, softened
225 g / 8 oz / 1 cup caster
   (superfine) sugar
4 large eggs, beaten
225 g / 8 oz / 1 ½ cups self-raising flour
2 tbsp unsweetened cocoa powder
100 g / 3 ½ oz milk chocolate, grated

1. Preheat the oven to 180°C (160°C fan) / 350F / gas 4 and grease and line a loaf tin with greaseproof paper.
2. Cream together the butter and sugar until well whipped then gradually whisk in the eggs, beating well after each addition.
3. Sift over the flour and cocoa powder and fold in with the grated chocolate.
4. Scrape the mixture into the tin and bake for 45 minutes or until a skewer inserted in the centre comes out clean.
5. Turn the loaf out onto a wire rack and leave to cool.

SERVES: 8-10 | PREP TIME: 5 MINS | COOKING TIME: 45-55 MINS

Raspberry and Coconut Cake

225 g / 8 oz / 1 cup butter, softened

225 g / 8 oz / 1 cup caster (superfine) sugar

4 large eggs, beaten

225 g/ 4 ½ oz / 1 ½ cups self-raising flour

100 g / 3 ½ oz / 1 cup desiccated coconut

150 g / 5 ½ oz / 1 cup raspberries

3 tbsp toasted coconut flakes

1. Preheat the oven to 180°C (160°C fan) / 350F / gas 4 and grease and line a 23 cm round cake tin with greaseproof paper.

2. Cream the butter and sugar together until well whipped then gradually whisk in the eggs, beating well after each addition.

3. Fold in the flour, desiccated coconut and raspberries then scrape the mixture into the tin. Sprinkle over the coconut flakes.

4. Bake the cake for 45–55 minutes or until a skewer inserted in the centre comes out clean.

5. Transfer the cake to a wire rack and leave to cool.

SERVES: **8** | PREP TIME: **15 MINS** | COOKING TIME: **55 MINS**

Summer Fruit Loaf Cake

225 g / 8oz / 1 ½ cups self-raising flour
100 g / 3 ½ oz / ½ cup butter, cubed
85 g / 3 oz / ⅓ cup caster (superfine) sugar
100 g / 3 ½ oz / ⅓ cup raspberries
100 g / 3 ½ oz / ⅔ cup blackberries
55 g / 2 oz / ⅔ cup redcurrants
1 large egg
75 ml / 2 ½ fl. oz / ⅓ cup whole milk

1. Preheat the oven to 180°C (160°C fan) / 350F / gas 4 and line a loaf tin with non-stick baking paper.
2. Sieve the flour into a mixing bowl and rub in the butter until it resembles fine breadcrumbs then stir in the sugar and fruit.
3. Lightly beat the egg with the milk and stir it into the dry ingredients until just combined.
4. Scrape the mixture into the loaf tin and bake for 55 minutes or until a skewer inserted in the centre comes out clean.
5. Transfer the cake to a wire rack and leave to cool completely.

SERVES: 10 | **PREP TIME: 10 MINS** | **COOKING TIME: 35-40 MINS**

Orange Drizzle Cake

150 g / 5 ½ oz / 1 cup self-raising flour
150 g / 5 ½ oz / ⅔ cup caster
  (superfine) sugar
150 g / 5 ½ oz / ⅔ cup butter
3 eggs
1 tsp baking powder
1 tbsp orange zest
2 tbsp orange juice

FOR THE DRIZZLE
100 g / 3 ½ oz / ½ cup caster
  (superfine) sugar
50 ml / 1 ¾ fl. oz / ¼ cup orange juice

1. Preheat the oven to 180°C (160°C fan) / 350F / gas 4 and grease and 20 cm round cake tin.
2. Put all of the cake ingredients in a large mixing bowl and whisk them together with an electric whisk for 4 minutes or until pale and well whipped.
3. Scrape the mixture into the tin and level the top with a spatula.
4. Bake for 35–40 minutes. While the cake is cooking, stir the caster sugar with the orange juice until dissolved.
5. The cake is ready when a toothpick inserted in the centre comes out clean. Spoon the orange drizzle all over the surface and leave it to cool in the tin.

Sweet Treats

SERVES: **8** | PREP TIME: **40 MINS** | COOKING TIME: **40-55 MINS**

Rhubarb and Custard Tart

3 sticks rhubarb, chopped
4 tbsp caster (superfine) sugar
icing (confectioner's) sugar to dust

FOR THE PASTRY
200 g / 7 oz / 1 ⅓ cups plain
   (all-purpose) flour
100 g / 3 ½ oz / ½ cup butter, cubed

FOR THE CUSTARD
4 large egg yolks
75 g / 2 ½ oz / ⅓ cup caster
   (superfine) sugar
1 tsp vanilla extract
2 tsp cornflour (cornstarch)
450 ml / 16 fl. oz / 1 ¾ cups whole milk

1. Preheat the oven to 200°C (180°C fan) / 400F / gas 6.
2. Put the rhubarb in a roasting tin and sprinkle with sugar then bake for 20 minutes or until tender.
3. Meanwhile, make the pastry. Rub the butter into the flour and add just enough cold water to bind.
4. Chill for 30 minutes then roll out on a floured surface. Use the pastry to line a rectangular tart tin.
5. Prick the pastry with a fork, line with cling film and fill with baking beans or rice.
6. Bake for 10 minutes then remove the cling film and baking beans and cook for another 8 minutes to crisp.
7. Reduce the oven temperature to 170°C (150°C fan) / 340F / gas 3.
8. Whisk together the custard ingredients and pour into the pastry case. Arrange the rhubarb on top.
9. Bake the tart for 25–35 minutes or until the custard is just set in the centre.
10. Leave to cool completely before dusting with icing sugar.

Black Sesame Tuiles

110 g / 4 oz / ⅔ cup plain (all-purpose)
  flour
110 g / 4 oz / ½ cup caster
  (superfine) sugar
2 large egg whites
110 g / 4 oz / ½ cup butter, melted
2 tbsp black sesame seeds

1. Beat together the flour, sugar and egg whites until smooth then beat in
   the melted butter and sesame seeds.
2. Refrigerate for 30 minutes.
3. Preheat the oven to 180°C (160°C fan) / 350F / gas 4 and oil 2 large
   baking trays.
4. Spoon teaspoonfuls of the mixture onto the baking trays and spread out with
   the back of the spoon to make 10 cm circles.
5. Bake the tuiles for 8-10 minutes then lift them off the trays with a palette knife
   and drape over a rolling pin while still soft. Leave to cool and harden.

Millionaire's Shortbread

230 g / 8 oz / 1 ½ cups plain (all-
  purpose) flour
2 tbsp cocoa powder
75 g / 2 ½ oz / ⅓ cup caster
  (superfine) sugar
150 g / 5 oz / ⅔ cup butter, cubed
50 g / 1 ¾ oz / ¼ cup granulated sugar
FOR THE TOPPING
1 can condensed milk
200 g / 7 oz milk chocolate

1. Make the caramel layer: put the unopened can of condensed milk in a pan
   of water and simmer for 3 hours, then leave the can to cool.
2. Preheat the oven to 180°C (160°C fan) / 350F / gas 4 and line a 20 cm square
   cake tin with greaseproof paper.
3. Mix the flour, cocoa and caster sugar in a bowl, then rub in the butter. Knead
   until the mixture forms a dough then press it evenly into the bottom of the tin.
4. Bake the shortbread for 15 minutes, then leave to cool. Open the condensed
   milk. Beat until smooth. Spread it over the shortbread and chill for 1 hour.
5. Melt the chocolate in a microwave and spread it over the caramel.
6. Chill in the fridge for 30 minutes.

MAKES: **6** | PREP TIME: **45 MINS** | COOKING TIME: **25-30 MINS**

Blueberry Tartlets

200 g / 7 oz blueberries

FOR THE PASTRY
200 g / 7 oz plain (all-purpose) flour
100 g / 3 ½ oz butter, cubed
1 egg, beaten

FOR THE CUSTARD
2 large egg yolks
55 g / 2 oz caster (superfine) sugar
1 tsp vanilla extract
2 tsp cornflour (cornstarch)
225 ml / 8 fl. oz / 1 cup whole milk

1. To make the pastry, rub the butter into the flour and add just enough cold water to bind. Chill for 30 minutes.
2. Preheat the oven to 200°C (180°C fan) / 400F / gas 6.
3. Roll out the pastry on a floured surface and use it to line 6 tartlet cases, re-rolling the trimmings as necessary.
4. Prick the pastry with a fork, line with cling film and fill with baking beans or rice. Bake for 10 minutes then remove the cling film and baking beans.
5. Brush the inside of the pastry cases with beaten egg and cook for another 8 minutes to crisp.
6. Whisk the custard ingredients together in a jug and ¾ fill the pastry cases.
7. Bake the tarts for 15–20 minutes or until the custard has set.
8. Leave the tartlets to cool completely before topping with the blueberries.

Milk Chocolate Fondants

2 tbsp unsweetened cocoa powder
150 g / 6 oz milk chocolate, chopped
150 g / 6 oz / ⅔ cup butter, chopped
85 g / 3 oz / ⅓ cup caster
  (superfine) sugar
3 large eggs
3 egg yolks
1 tbsp plain (all-purpose) flour

1. Oil 6 mini pudding basins and dust the insides with cocoa.
2. Melt the chocolate, butter and sugar together in a saucepan, stirring to dissolve the sugar.
3. Leave to cool a little then beat in the eggs and egg yolks and fold in the flour.
4. Divide the mixture between the pudding basins and chill them for 30 minutes.
5. Preheat the oven to 180°C (160°C fan) / 350F / gas 4 and put a baking tray in to heat.
6. Transfer the fondants to the heated baking tray and bake in the oven for 8 minutes.
7. Leave the fondants to cool for 2 minutes, then turn them out of their moulds and serve immediately.

Raspberry Sponge Squares

175 g / 6 oz / 1 ¼ cup self-raising flour
2 tsp baking powder
175 g / 6 oz / ¾ cup caster (superfine) sugar
175 g / 6 oz / ¾ cup butter
3 eggs
200 g / 7 oz / 1 ⅓ cups raspberries
icing (confectioner's) sugar to dust

1. Preheat the oven to 180°C (160°C fan) / 350F / gas 4 and grease and line a square cake tin.
2. Put the flour, baking powder, sugar, butter and eggs in a mixing bowl and whisk them together with an electric whisk for 4 minutes or until pale.
3. Arrange the raspberries in the bottom of the cake tin and spoon over the cake mixture.
4. Bake for 30–35 minutes. The cake is ready when a toothpick inserted in the centre comes out clean.
5. Transfer the cake to a wire rack to cool completely before dusting with icing sugar and cutting into squares.

Summer Fruit Meringue Roulade

4 large egg whites
a pinch cream of tartar
200 g / 7 oz / ¾ cup caster (superfine) sugar
300 ml / 10 ½ fl. oz / 1 ¼ cups double (heavy) cream
200 g / 7 oz / 1 ⅓ cups mixed berries
icing (confectioner's) sugar for dusting

1. Preheat the oven to 180°C (160°C fan) / 350F / gas 4 and line a Swiss roll tin with non-stick baking paper.
2. Whisk the egg whites with the cream of tartar until stiff then whisk in the caster sugar a tablespoon at a time.
3. Spread it onto the Swiss roll tray in an even layer with a palette knife and bake for 15 minutes.
4. Leave to cool completely.
5. Whip the double cream until it just holds its shape.
6. Sprinkle a large sheet of greaseproof paper with icing sugar and turn the meringue out onto it.
7. Spread the meringue with cream and sprinkle over the berries then roll it up, using the greaseproof paper to help you.
8. Dust with more icing sugar before serving.

Chocolate and Pear Tarte Tatin

2 tbsp butter
2 tbsp dark brown sugar
6 pears, peeled, cored and halved
250 g / 9 oz all-butter puff pastry
100 g / 3 ½ oz dark chocolate (minimum 60 % cocoa solids), chopped

1. Preheat the oven to 220°C (200°C fan) / 425F / gas 7.
2. Heat the butter and sugar in an ovenproof pan and add the pears. Cook over a low heat for 5 minutes, turning occasionally, until they start to soften.
3. Arrange the pears, cut side up and leave to cool a little.
4. Roll out the pastry on a floured surface and cut out a circle the same size as the frying pan.
5. Lay the pastry over the pears and tuck in the edges, then transfer the pan to the oven and bake for 25 minutes or until the pastry is golden brown.
6. Meanwhile, melt the chocolate in a microwave or bain-marie.
7. Using oven gloves, put a large plate on top of the frying pan and turn them both over in one smooth movement to unmould the tart.
8. Drizzle the melted chocolate between the pears and serve immediately.

MAKES: **1 LOAF** | PREP TIME: **2 HOURS 30 MINS** | COOKING TIME: **35-40 MINS**

Hot Cross Bun Loaf

55 g / 2 oz / ¼ cup butter, cubed
400 g / 14 oz / 2 ⅔ cups strong white bread flour, plus extra for dusting
½ tsp easy-blend dried yeast
4 tbsp caster (superfine) sugar
1 tsp fine sea salt
2 tsp mixed spice
100 g / 3 ½ oz / ½ cup mixed dried fruit
4 tbsp plain (all-purpose) flour
1 egg, beaten

1. Rub the butter into the bread flour and stir in the yeast, sugar, salt and spice. Stir the dried fruit into 280ml of warm water and stir into the dry ingredients.
2. Knead the mixture on a lightly oiled surface for 10 minutes or until the dough is smooth and elastic.
3. Leave the dough to rest, covered with a lightly oiled bowl, for 1–2 hours or until doubled in size.
4. Roll the dough into a fat sausage. Turn it 90°C and roll it tightly the other way then tuck the ends under and transfer to the tin. Leave to prove for 45 minutes.
5. Preheat the oven to 220°C (200°C fan) / 425F / gas 7.
6. Mix the plain flour with just enough water to make a thick paste and spoon it into a piping bag. Brush the loaf with egg and pipe the flour mixture on top into crosses.
7. Bake for 35–40 minutes or until the underneath sounds hollow when tapped.

MAKES: 6 | PREP TIME: 30 MINS | COOKING TIME: 20 MINS

Apple and Walnut Tartlets

225 g / 8 oz puff pastry
150 g / 5 ½ oz / 1 ½ cups
    ground walnuts
150 g / 5 ½ oz / ⅔ cup butter, softened
150 g / 5 ½ oz / ⅔ cup caster
    (superfine) sugar
2 large eggs
2 tbsp plain (all-purpose) flour
4 eating apples, cored and sliced
4 tbsp runny honey
2 tbsp chopped walnuts

1. Preheat the oven to 200°C (180°C fan) / 400F / gas 6.
2. Roll out the pastry on a floured surface and use it to line 6 round loose-bottomed tartlet cases.
3. Prick the pastry with a fork, line with greaseproof paper and fill with baking beans or rice.
4. Bake for 10 minutes then remove the paper and baking beans.
5. Whisk together the ground walnuts, butter, sugar, eggs and flour until smoothly whipped and spoon the mixture into the pastry case.
6. Arrange the apple slices on top and bake for 20 minutes or until the frangipane is cooked through and the pastry is crisp underneath.
7. Heat the honey until very liquid and stir in the walnuts then drizzle it over the hot tarts.
8. Serve warm with clotted cream or ice cream.

Lemon and Almond Shortbread Biscuits

175 g / 6 oz / 1 cup plain (all-purpose) flour
55 g / 2 oz / ½ cup ground almonds
75 g / 2 ½ oz / ⅓ cup caster (superfine) sugar
150 g / 5 oz / ⅔ cup butter, cubed
1 lemon, zest finely grated
50 g / 1 ¾ oz / ¼ cup granulated sugar

1. Preheat the oven to 180°C (160°C fan) 350F / gas 4 and line a baking tray with greaseproof paper.
2. Mix together the flour, ground almonds and caster sugar in a bowl, then rub in the butter and lemon zest.
3. Knead gently until the mixture forms a smooth dough then form into cylinder 6 cm in diameter and roll in granulated sugar.
4. Slice the roll into 1 cm thick slices and spread them out on the baking tray.
5. Bake the biscuits for 15–20 minutes, turning the tray round halfway through.
6. Transfer the biscuits to a wire rack and leave to cool.

Quinoa Biscuits

150 g / 5 ½ oz / 1 ½ cup quinoa flakes
50 g / 1 ¾ oz / ½ cup porridge oats
125 g / 4 ½ oz / ¾ cup stoneground wholemeal flour
1 tsp baking powder
175 g / 6 oz / ¾ cup butter
150 g / 5 ½ oz / ¾ cup soft brown sugar
110 g / 4 oz / ½ cup raw quinoa

1. Put the quinoa flakes, oats, flour and baking powder in a food processor and blitz until fine.
2. Cream the butter with the sugar then beat in the dry ingredients.
3. Bring the dough together and shape into a log then chill for 30 minutes.
4. Preheat the oven to 180°C (160°C fan) / 350F / gas 4 and line 2 baking sheets with greaseproof paper.
5. Slice the log into 1 cm slices and roll in the raw quinoa to coat.
6. Transfer the biscuits to the prepared trays and bake for 20–25 minutes or until cooked through and golden brown.
7. Transfer the biscuits to a wire rack and leave to cool completely.

SERVES: 8 | **PREP TIME: 25 MINS** | **COOKING TIME: 15-20 MINS**

Rich Chocolate Tart

250 ml / 9 fl. oz / 1 cup double cream

250 g / 9 oz dark chocolate (minimum 60 % cocoa solids), chopped

55 g / 2 oz / ¼ cup butter, softened

FOR THE PASTRY

100 g / 3 ½ oz / ½ cup butter, cubed

200 g / 7 oz / 1 ⅓ cup plain (all-purpose) flour

55 g / 2 oz / ¼ cup caster (superfine) sugar

1 egg, beaten

1. Preheat the oven to 200°C (180°C fan) / 400F / gas 6.

2. To make the pastry, rub the butter into the flour and sugar and add the egg with just enough cold water to bind.

3. Wrap the dough in cling film and chill for 30 minutes then roll out on a floured surface.

4. Use the pastry to line a 23 cm loose-bottomed tart tin and trim the edges.

5. Prick the pastry with a fork, line with cling film and fill with baking beans or rice.

6. Bake for 10 minutes then remove the cling film and baking beans and cook for another 8 minutes to crisp.

7. Heat the cream to simmering point then pour it over the chocolate and stir until smooth.

8. Add the butter and blend it in with a stick blender.

9. Pour the ganache into the pastry case and level the top with a palette knife.

10. Leave the ganache to cool and set for at least 2 hours before cutting and serving.

MAKES: **36** | PREP TIME: **10 MINS** | COOKING TIME: **12-15 MINS**

Ginger Snap Biscuits

75 g / 2 ½ oz / ⅓ cup butter, softened
100 g / 3 ½ oz / ⅓ cup golden syrup
225 g / 8 oz / 1 ½ cups self-raising flour
100 g / 3 ½ oz / ½ cup caster (superfine) sugar
1 tsp ground ginger
1 large egg, beaten

1. Preheat the oven to 180°C (160°C fan) / 350F / gas 4 and line 2 baking sheets with greaseproof paper.
2. Melt the butter and golden syrup together in a saucepan.
3. Mix the flour, sugar and ground ginger together then stir in the melted butter mixture and the beaten egg.
4. Use a teaspoon to portion the mixture onto the baking trays, leaving plenty of room for the biscuits to spread.
5. Bake in batches for 12–15 minutes or until golden brown.
6. Transfer the biscuits to a wire rack and leave to cool and harden.

SERVES: 6 | PREP TIME: 10 MINS | COOKING TIME: 35-45 MINS

Grape Clafoutis

75 g / 2 ½ oz / ⅓ cup caster (superfine) sugar
75 g / 2 ½ oz / ⅓ cup butter
300 ml / 10 ½ fl. oz / 1 ¼ cups whole milk
2 large eggs
50 g / 1 ¾ oz / ⅓ cup plain (all-purpose) flour
2 tbsp ground almonds
1 lemon, zest finely grated
300 g / 10 ½ oz / 2 cups mixed seedless grapes

1. Preheat the oven to 190°C (170°C fan) / 375F / gas 5.
2. Melt the butter in a saucepan and cook over a low heat until it starts to smell nutty.
3. Brush a little of the butter around the inside of a 20 cm round pie dish then add a spoonful of caster sugar and shake to coat.
4. Whisk together the milk and eggs with the rest of the butter.
5. Sift the flour into a mixing bowl with a pinch of salt and stir in the ground almonds, lemon zest and the rest of the sugar.
6. Make a well in the middle of the dry ingredients and gradually whisk in the liquid, incorporating all the flour from around the outside until you have a lump-free batter.
7. Arrange the grapes in the prepared pie dish, pour over the batter and transfer to the oven immediately.
8. Bake the clafoutis for 35–45 minutes or until a skewer inserted in the centre comes out clean.
9. Serve warm or at room temperature.

Almond and White Chocolate Blondies

110 g / 4 oz white chocolate, chopped
225 g / 8 oz / 1 cup butter
450 g / 15 oz / 2 ½ cups light brown sugar
4 large eggs
110 g / 4 oz / ⅔ cup self-raising flour
110 g / 4 oz / ⅔ cup almonds

1. Preheat the oven to 170°C (150°C fan) / 340F / gas 3 and oil and line a 20 x 20 cm square cake tin.
2. Melt the chocolate and butter together in a saucepan, then leave to cool a little.
3. Whisk the sugar and eggs together with an electric whisk for 3 minutes or until very light and creamy.
4. Pour in the chocolate mixture and sieve over the flour, then fold everything together with the almonds until evenly mixed.
5. Scrape into the tin and bake for 35–40 minutes or until the outside is set, but the centre is still quite soft, as it will continue to cook as it cools.
6. Leave the blondie to cool completely before cutting into 9 squares.

Plum Tartlets

110 g / 4 oz / ½ cup butter, cubed and chilled
110 g / 4 oz / ⅔ cup plain (all-purpose) flour
110 g / 4 oz / ⅔ cup stoneground wholemeal flour
450 g / 1 lb plums, halved and stoned
450 g / 1 lb / 1 ¼ cup plum jam (jelly)

1. Preheat the oven to 200°C (180°C fan) / 400F / gas 6.
2. Rub the butter into the flours until the mixture resembles fine breadcrumbs.
3. Stir in just enough cold water to bring the pastry together into a pliable dough.
4. Roll out the pastry on a floured surface and cut out 6 circles then use them to line 6 tartlet tins.
5. Arrange the halved plums in the pastry case and spoon over the jam.
6. Bake for 25–35 minutes or until the pastry is crisp and the jam has melted around the plums.

SERVES: 8 | PREP TIME: 55 MINS | COOKING TIME: 25-30 MINS

Lemon Meringue Pie

2 tsp cornflour (cornstarch)
4 lemons, zest and juice
4 large eggs, beaten
225 g / 8 oz / 1 cup butter
175 g / 6 oz / ¾ cups caster (superfine) sugar

FOR THE PASTRY
100 g / 3 ½ oz / ½ cups butter, cubed
200 g / 7 oz / 1 ⅓ cups plain (all-purpose) flour

FOR THE MERINGUE
4 large egg whites
110g / 4 oz / ½ cups caster (superfine) sugar

1. Preheat the oven to 200°C (180°C fan) / 400F / gas 6.
2. Rub the butter into the flour and add just enough cold water to bind.
3. Chill for 30 minutes then roll out on a floured surface.
4. Use the pastry to line a 24 cm loose-bottomed tart tin and prick it with a fork.
5. Line the pastry with cling film and fill with baking beans or rice then bake for 10 minutes.
6. Remove the cling film and beans and cook for another 8 minutes to crisp.
7. Meanwhile, dissolve the cornflour in the lemon juice and put it in a saucepan with the rest of the ingredients.
8. Stir constantly over a medium heat to melt the butter and dissolve the sugar. Bring to a gentle simmer then pour it into the pastry case.
9. Whisk the egg whites until stiff, then gradually add the sugar and whisk until the mixture is thick and shiny.
10. Spoon the meringue on top of the lemon curd, making peaks with the spoon.
11. Bake for 10 minutes or until golden brown.

SERVES: **8** | PREP TIME: **40 MINS** | COOKING TIME: **40-50 MINS**

Wholemeal Raspberry Custard Tart

200 g / 7 oz / 1 ⅓ cups raspberries

FOR THE PASTRY
100 g / 3 ½ oz / cup butter, cubed
200 g / 7 oz / 1 ⅓ cups stoneground
  wholemeal flour

FOR THE CUSTARD
4 large egg yolks
75 g / 2 ½ oz / ⅓ cup caster
  (superfine) sugar
1 tsp vanilla extract
2 tsp cornflour (cornstarch)
450 ml / 16 fl. oz / 1 cups whole milk

1. Preheat the oven to 200°C (180°C fan) / 400F / gas 6.
2. Rub the butter into the flour and add just enough cold water to bind.
3. Chill for 30 minutes then roll out on a floured surface. Use the pastry to
   line a 23 cm round tart tin.
4. Prick the pastry with a fork, line with cling film and fill with baking beans or rice.
5. Bake for 10 minutes then remove the cling film and baking beans and cook
   for another 8 minutes to crisp.
6. Reduce the oven temperature to 170°C (150°C fan) / 340F / gas 3.
7. Whisk together the custard ingredients and pour into the pastry case.
   Arrange the raspberries on top.
8. Bake the tart for 25–35 minutes or until the custard is just set in the centre.

SERVES: **8** | PREP TIME: **20-25 MINS** | CHILLING TIME: **4 HOURS**

Chocolate and Cherry Summer Pudding

300 g / 10 ½ oz / 2 cups cherries, stoned and halved
4 tbsp caster (superfine) sugar
1 tbsp kirsch
6 slices white bread, crusts removed
250 ml / 9 fl. oz / 1 cup double (heavy) cream
250 g / 9 oz dark chocolate (minimum 60 % cocoa solids), chopped

1. Put the cherries in a bowl with the sugar and kirsch and leave to macerate for 2 hours. Line a pudding basin with cling film.
2. Put the cherries in a sieve and collect the juice.
3. Dip the bread in the cherry juice and use it to line the pudding basin, saving one slice for the lid.
4. Bring the cream to a simmer then pour it over the chocolate and stir gently to emulsify.
5. Fold the cherries into the chocolate ganache and spoon it into the pudding basin.
6. Top with the last slice of soaked bread then cover the basin with cling film.
7. Put a small board on top of the pudding basin and weigh it down with a can, then leave it to chill in the fridge for at least 4 hours.
8. Invert the pudding onto a plate and peel away the cling film.

Fresh Fruit Sponge Pudding

110 g / 4 oz / ⅔ cup self-raising
  flour, sifted
110 g / 4 oz / ½ cup caster (superfine)
  sugar
110 g / 4 oz / ½ cup butter, softened
2 large eggs
1 tsp vanilla extract
2 plums, cut into eighths
55 g / 1 oz / ⅓ cup raspberries
55 g / 1 oz / ⅓ cup seedless black grapes

1. Preheat the oven to 190°C (170°C fan) / 375F / gas 5 and butter a small baking dish.
2. Combine the flour, sugar, butter, eggs and vanilla extract in a bowl and whisk together for 2 minutes or until smooth.
3. Arrange half of the fruit in the baking dish and spoon in the cake mixture.
4. Top with the rest of the fruit then bake for 30–35 minutes.
5. Test with a wooden toothpick; if it comes out clean, the cake is done.
6. Serve warm with custard or cream.

Summer Berry Chocolate Brownies

110 g / 4 oz dark chocolate (minimum
  60 % cocoa solids), chopped
85 g / 3 oz / ¾ cup unsweetened cocoa
  powder, sifted
225 g / 8 oz / 1 cup butter
450 g / 15 oz / 2 ½ cups light brown sugar
4 large eggs
110 g / 4 oz / ⅔ cup self-raising flour
175 g / 6 oz / 1 ¼ cups mixed berries

1. Preheat the oven to 170°C (150°C fan) / 340F / gas 3 and oil and line a 20 x 20 cm square cake tin.
2. Melt the chocolate, cocoa and butter together in a saucepan, then leave to cool a little.
3. Whisk the sugar and eggs together with an electric whisk for 3 minutes or until very light and creamy.
4. Pour in the chocolate mixture and sieve over the flour. Reserve some of the berries for decoration and add the rest to the bowl, then fold everything together until evenly mixed.
5. Scrape into the tin and bake for 35–40 minutes or until the outside is set, but the centre is still quite soft, as it will continue to cook as it cools.
6. Leave the brownie to cool completely before cutting into 9 squares.

SERVES: **8** | PREP TIME: **25 MINS** | COOKING TIME: **35-45 MINS**

Almond Filo Pie

450 g / 1 lb filo pastry
200 g / 7 oz / ¾ cup butter, melted
450 g / 1 lb / 3 cups blanched almonds
100 g / 3 ½ oz / ½ cup caster
   (superfine) sugar
1 lemon, zest finely grated
icing (confectioner's) sugar to dust

1. Preheat the oven to 180°C
   (160°C fan) / 350F / gas 4 and
   butter a round baking dish.
2. Brush 10 sheets of filo pastry with
   melted butter and use to line the
   baking dish.
3. Put the almonds, sugar and lemon
   zest in a food processor and pulse
   until finely chopped.
4. Add half of the remaining butter
   and pulse again.
5. Spread a third of the almond
   mixture across the bottom of the
   pastry case.
6. Top with a third of the remaining
   pastry sheets, making sure each
   one is well buttered.
7. Continue layering, finishing with
   a layer of buttered filo, then fold
   in the edges to neaten.
8. Bake the pie in the oven for
   35–45 minutes or until the pastry
   is golden and cooked through in
   the centre.
9. Unmould the pie and dust liberally
   with icing sugar.

SERVES: **6** | PREP TIME: **10 MINS** | COOKING TIME: **35-45 MINS**

Cherry Clafoutis

300 g / 10 ½ oz / 2 cups cherries, stoned
2 tbsp kirsch
75 g / 2 ½ oz / ⅓ cup butter
75 g / 2 ½ oz / ⅓ cup caster (superfine) sugar
300 ml / 10 ½ fl. oz / 1 ¼ cups whole milk
2 large eggs
50 g / 1 ¾ oz / ⅓ cup plain (all-purpose) flour
2 tbsp ground almonds

1. Preheat the oven to 190°C (170°C fan) / 375F / gas 5.
2. Put the cherries in a bowl with the kirsch and leave to marinate for 30 minutes.
3. Melt the butter in a saucepan and cook over a low heat until it starts to smell nutty.
4. Brush a little of the butter around the inside of a 20 cm quiche dish then add a spoonful of caster sugar and shake to coat.
5. Whisk together the milk and eggs with the rest of the butter.
6. Sift the flour into a mixing bowl with a pinch of salt and stir in the ground almonds and the rest of the sugar.
7. Make a well in the middle of the dry ingredients and gradually whisk in the liquid, incorporating all the flour from round the outside until you have a lump-free batter.
8. Arrange the cherries in the prepared baking dish, pour over the batter and transfer to the oven immediately.
9. Bake the clafoutis for 35–45 minutes or until a skewer inserted in the centre comes out clean.
10. Leave to cool and serve warm or at room temperature.

Pear and Almond Tart

150 g / 5 ½ oz / 1 ½ cups ground almonds
150 g / 5 ½ oz / ⅔ cup butter, softened
150 g / 5 ½ oz / ⅔ cup caster (superfine) sugar
2 large eggs
2 tbsp plain (all-purpose) flour
1 pastry case
4 pears, cored and quartered
4 tbsp apricot jam (jelly)
2 tbsp flaked (slivered) almonds

1. Preheat the oven to 200°C (180°C fan) / 400F / gas 6.
2. Whisk together the almonds, butter, sugar, eggs and flour until smoothly whipped and spoon the mixture into the pastry case.
3. Press the pear quarters into the frangipane and bake the tart for 25 minutes or until the frangipane is cooked through.
4. Heat the apricot jam until runny and brush it over the pears then sprinkle with flaked almonds.

Chocolate and Sponge Biscuit Brownies

110 g / 4 oz milk chocolate, chopped
85 g / 3 oz / ¾ cup cocoa powder, sifted
225 g / 8 oz / 1 cup butter
450 g / 15 oz / 2 ½ cups light brown sugar
4 large eggs
110 g / 4 oz / ⅔ cup self-raising flour
8 sponge finger biscuits, broken into pieces

1. Preheat the oven to 170°C (150°C fan) / 340F / gas 3 and oil and line a 20 x 20 cm square cake tin.
2. Melt the chocolate, cocoa and butter together in a saucepan, then leave to cool a little.
3. Whisk the sugar and eggs together with an electric whisk for 3 minutes or until very light and creamy.
4. Pour in the chocolate mixture and sieve over the flour, then fold everything together with the sponge finger biscuits until evenly mixed.
5. Scrape into the tin and bake for 35–40 minutes or until a skewer inserted comes out clean.
6. Leave the brownie to cool completely before cutting into 9 squares.

MAKES: **12** | PREP TIME: **4 HOURS 30 MINS** | COOKING TIME: **10-15 MINS**

Brioche Cream Buns

250 g / 9 oz / 1 ¼ cups butter, cubed
400 g / 14 oz / 2 ⅔ cups strong white
  bread flour
2 ½ tsp easy blend dried yeast
4 tbsp caster (superfine) sugar
1 tsp fine sea salt
4 large eggs, plus 3 extra yolks

TO FINISH
1 egg, beaten
4 tbsp sugar nibs
300 ml / 10 ½ fl. oz / 1 ¼ cups
  whipped cream

1. Rub the butter into the flour then
   stir in the yeast, sugar and salt.
   Beat the whole eggs and yolks
   together and stir into the dry
   ingredients.
2. Knead the dough on a lightly oiled
   surface with 2 plastic scrapers for
   10 minutes until smooth.
3. Leave the dough to rest in a lightly
   oiled bowl, covered with oiled cling
   film, for 2 hours.
4. Divide the dough into 12 balls
   and transfer them to a greased
   baking tray.
5. Cover with oiled cling film and
   leave to prove for 2 hours or until
   doubled in size.
6. Meanwhile, preheat the oven to
   220°C (200°C fan) / 425F / gas 7.
   Once risen, brush the tops with
   beaten egg and sprinkle with sugar
   nibs then bake for 10–15 minutes.
7. Transfer the rolls to a wire rack
   and leave to cool completely
   before splitting and filling with
   whipped cream.

MAKES: **12** | PREP TIME: **1 HOUR 30 MINS** | COOKING TIME: **10-15 MINS**

Lemon Madeleines

110 g / 4 oz / ½ cup butter

55 g / 2 oz / ⅓ cup plain (all-purpose) flour

1 lemon, zest finely grated

55 g / 2 oz / ½ cup ground almonds

110 g / 4 oz / 1 cup icing (confectioner's) sugar

3 large egg whites

1. Heat the butter until it foams and starts to smell nutty then leave to cool.

2. Combine the flour, lemon zest, ground almonds and the icing sugar in a bowl and whisk in the eggs whites.

3. Pour the cooled butter into the bowl and whisk into the mixture until evenly mixed.

4. Leave the cake mixture to rest in the fridge for an hour.

5. Preheat the oven to 170°C (150°C fan) / 325F / gas 3 and oil and flour a 12-hole Madeleine mould.

6. Spoon the mixture into the moulds, then transfer the tin to the oven and bake for 10–15 minutes.

7. Test with a wooden toothpick; if it comes out clean, the cakes are done.

8. Transfer the cakes to a wire rack to cool for 5 minutes before serving.

MAKES: **6** | PREP TIME: **45 MINS** | COOKING TIME: **15-20 MINS**

Strawberry and Custard Tartlets

200 g / 7 oz / 1 ⅓ cups strawberries, sliced
For the pastry
200 g / 7 oz / 1 ⅓ cups plain (all-purpose) flour
100 g / 3 ½ oz / ½ cup butter, cubed

FOR THE CUSTARD
2 large egg yolks
55 g / 2 oz / ¼ cup caster (superfine) sugar
1 tsp vanilla extract
2 tsp cornflour (cornstarch)
225 ml / 8 fl. oz / ¾ cup whole milk

1. To make the pastry, rub the butter into the flour and add just enough cold water to bind.
2. Chill for 30 minutes.
3. Preheat the oven to 200°C (180°C fan) / 400F / gas 6.
4. Roll out the pastry on a floured surface and use it to line 6 tartlet cases, rerolling the trimmings as necessary.
5. Arrange the strawberry slices in the pastry cases.
6. Whisk the custard ingredients together in a jug and ¾ fill the pastry cases.
7. Bake the tarts for 15–20 minutes or until the custard has set and the pastry is crisp.

Wholemeal Oat Cookies

175 g / 6 oz / ¾ cup butter, melted
225 g / 8 oz / 1 ⅓ cup dark brown sugar
100 g / 3 ½ oz / ½ cup caster
(superfine) sugar
2 tsp vanilla extract
1 egg, plus 1 egg yolk
125 g / 4 ½ oz / ¾ cup self-raising flour
125 g / 4 ½ oz / ¾ cup stoneground
wholemeal flour
125 g / 4 ½ oz / 1 ¼ cup oats

1. Preheat the oven to 170°C (150°C fan) / 340F / gas 3 and line two baking sheets with greaseproof paper.
2. Cream together the two sugars, butter and vanilla extract until pale and well whipped then beat in the egg and yolk, followed by the flours and oats.
3. Drop tablespoons of the mixture onto the prepared trays, leaving plenty of room to spread.
4. Bake the cookies in batches for 12–15 minutes or until the edges are starting to brown, but the centres are still chewy.
5. Transfer to a wire rack and leave to cool.

Chocolate Brownies

110 g / 4 oz milk chocolate, chopped
85 g / 3 oz / ¾ cup unsweetened cocoa
powder, sifted
225 g / 8 oz / 1 cup butter
450 g /15 oz / 2 ½ cups light brown sugar
4 large eggs
110 g / 4 oz / ⅔ cup self-raising flour

1. Preheat the oven to 170°C (150°C fan) / 340F / gas 3 and oil and line a 20 x 20 cm square cake tin.
2. Melt the chocolate, cocoa and butter together in a saucepan, then leave to cool a little.
3. Whisk the sugar and eggs together with an electric whisk for 3 minutes or until very light and creamy.
4. Pour in the chocolate mixture and sieve over the flour, then fold everything together until evenly mixed.
5. Scrape into the tin and bake for 35–40 minutes or until the outside is set, but the centre is still quite soft, as it will continue to cook as it cools.
6. Leave the brownie to cool completely before cutting into 9 squares.

MAKES: 6 | **PREP TIME: 45 MINS** | **COOKING TIME: 25-30 MINS**

Orange Custard Tartlets

FOR THE PASTRY
200 g / 7 oz / 1 ⅓ cups plain
  (all-purpose) flour
100 g / 3 ½ oz / ½ cup butter, cubed

FOR THE CUSTARD
2 large egg yolks
55 g / 2 oz / ¼ cup caster
  (superfine) sugar
2 tsp cornflour (cornstarch)
125 ml / 4 ½ fl. oz / ½ cup whole milk
100 ml / 3 ½ fl. oz / ½ cup fresh
  orange juice, sieved
1 tbsp orange zest, finely grated

1. To make the pastry, rub the butter into the flour and add just enough cold water to bind.
2. Chill for 30 minutes.
3. Preheat the oven to 200°C (180°C fan) / 400F / gas 6.
4. Roll out the pastry on a floured surface and use it to line 6 tartlet cases, rerolling the trimmings as necessary.
5. Prick the pastry with a fork, line with cling film and fill with baking beans or rice.
6. Bake for 10 minutes then remove the cling film and baking beans.
7. Whisk the custard ingredients together in a jug and ¾ fill the pastry cases.
8. Bake the tarts for 15–20 minutes or until the custard has set and the pastry is crisp.

MAKES: **6** | PREP TIME: **45 MINS** | COOKING TIME: **18 MINS**

Summer Berry and Mascarpone Tartlets

450 g / 1 lb / 2 cups mascarpone
100 g / 3 ½ oz / 1 cup icing
  (confectioner's) sugar
1 tsp vanilla extract
12 strawberries, halved
12 raspberries
100 g / 3 ½ oz / ⅔ cup blueberries
6 sprigs redcurrants

FOR THE PASTRY
200 g / 7 oz / 1 ⅓ cups plain (all-
  purpose) flour
100 g / 3 ½ oz / ½ cup butter, cubed
1 egg, beaten

1. Preheat the oven to 200°C
   (180°C fan) / 400F / gas 6.
2. To make the pastry, rub the butter
   into the flour and add just enough
   cold water to bind.
3. Chill for 30 minutes then roll out
   on a floured surface. Use the
   pastry to line 6 tartlet cases.
4. Prick the pastry with a fork, line
   with cling film and fill with baking
   beans or rice.
5. Bake for 10 minutes then remove
   the cling film and baking beans.
6. Brush the inside of the pastry cases
   with beaten egg and cook for
   another 8 minutes to crisp.
7. Whisk the mascarpone with the
   icing sugar and vanilla extract
   until smooth.
8. When the pastry cases have cooled
   to room temperature, spoon in the
   filling and level the tops.
9. Arrange the fruit on top of the
   filling and serve.

SERVES: 6 | PREP TIME: 15 MINS | COOKING TIME: 25-30 MINS

Chocolate, Orange and Almond Torte

2 large eggs, separated
150 g / 5 ½ oz / ⅔ cup caster
  (superfine) sugar
75 g / 2 ½ oz / ⅓ cup butter
2 tbsp unsweetened cocoa powder
100 g / 3 ½ oz dark chocolate (minimum
  60% cocoa solids), chopped
150 g / 5 ½ oz / 1 ½ cups ground
  almonds
1 orange, zest finely grated

TO DECORATE
100 g / 3 ½ oz / ½ cup caster
  (superfine) sugar
6 almonds
1 orange, zest finely pared

1. Preheat the oven to 180°C (160°C fan) / 350F / gas 4 and line a round
   spring-form cake tin.
2. Whisk the egg yolks and sugar together for 4 minutes.
3. Melt the butter, cocoa and chocolate together then fold into the egg yolk
   mixture with the ground almonds.
4. Whip the egg whites to stiff peaks in a very clean bowl and fold them into
   the cake mixture.
5. Scrape the mixture into the tin, being careful to retain as many air bubbles
   as possible, and bake for 25–30 minutes or until the centre is just set.
6. Transfer to a wire rack to cool. Heat the sugar in a small saucepan until it
   has all dissolved and turned a light caramel colour.
7. Use a fork to dip the almonds and orange zest in the caramel and leave
   them to set on a non-stick baking mat.
8. Cut the torte into wedges and decorate with the caramel almonds and
   orange zest.

Bread and Savoury Bakes

MAKES: **12** | PREP TIME: **2 HOURS 30 MINS** | COOKING TIME: **15-20 MINS**

Crusty Farmhouse Rolls

350 g / 12 ½ oz/ 2 ⅓ cups strong white
   bread flour, plus extra for dusting
50 g / 1 ¾ oz / ⅓ cup stoneground
   wholemeal flour
½ tsp easy-blend dried yeast
1 tbsp caster (superfine) sugar
1 tsp fine sea salt
1 tbsp olive oil

1. Mix together the flours, yeast,
   sugar and salt. Stir in the oil and
   280ml of warm water.

2. Knead the mixture on a lightly
   oiled surface with your hands for
   10 minutes or until smooth
   and elastic.

3. Leave the dough to rest in an
   oiled bowl, covered with oiled
   cling film, for 2 hours. Knead it for
   2 more minutes then split into
   12 even pieces and shape into rolls.

4. Transfer the rolls to a greased
   baking tray and cover with oiled
   cling film. Leave to prove for
   1 hour.

5. Meanwhile, preheat the oven to
   220°C (200°C fan) / 425F / gas 7.

6. Dust the rolls with flour and slash
   the tops with a knife.

7. Transfer the tray to the top shelf of
   the oven then quickly throw a small
   cupful of water onto the oven floor
   and close the door.

8. Bake for 15–20 minutes or until the
   rolls sound hollow when you tap
   them underneath.

9. Transfer to a wire rack and leave
   to cool.

MAKES: 1 LOAF | PREP TIME: 2 HOURS 30 MINS | COOKING TIME: 35-40 MINS

Wholemeal Sun-dried Tomato Bread

200 g / 7 oz / 1 ⅓ cup strong white bread flour, plus extra for dusting
200 g / 7 oz / 1 ⅓ cup stoneground wholemeal flour
½ tsp easy-blend dried yeast
1 tbsp caster (superfine) sugar
1 tsp fine sea salt
150 g / 5 ½ oz / ¾ cup sun-dried tomatoes in oil, drained
1 tbsp olive oil

1. Mix together the flours, yeast, sugar, salt and tomatoes.
2. Stir in the oil and 280ml warm water. Knead the mixture on a lightly oiled surface for 10 minutes or until smooth and elastic. Leave the dough to rest in an oiled bowl for 1–2 hours.
3. Roll the dough with your hands into a fat sausage, then turn it 90°C and roll it tightly the other way. Tuck the ends under and transfer the dough to the tin, keeping the seam underneath.
4. Cover the tin loosely with oiled cling film and leave to prove somewhere warm for 45 minutes.
5. Preheat the oven to 220°C (200°C fan) / 425F / gas 7.
6. Transfer the tin to the top shelf of the oven then quickly throw a small cupful of water onto the floor of the oven and close the door.
7. Bake for 35–40 minutes or until the loaf sounds hollow when you tap it underneath.

Cheese Wafer Biscuits

225 g / 8 oz / 1 cup butter
½ tsp cayenne pepper
175 g / 6 oz / 1 ¾ cups Red Leicester
cheese, grated
300 g / 10 ½ oz / 2 cups plain
(all-purpose) flour

1. Preheat the oven to 180°C (160°C fan) / 350F / gas 4 and line 2 baking sheets with greaseproof paper.
2. Melt the butter with the cayenne pepper in a saucepan.
3. Stir in the cheese and flour, beating rapidly to form a paste.
4. Use a teaspoon to portion the mixture onto the baking trays and spread the biscuits out thinly with the back of the spoon.
5. Bake in batches for 8–10 minutes.
6. Leave the biscuits to harden on the tray for a few minutes then transfer them to a wire rack to cool.

Wholemeal Cob Loaf

300 g / 10 ½ oz / 2 cup stoneground
wholemeal flour
100 g / 3 ½ oz / ½ cup strong white
bread flour, plus extra for dusting
½ tsp easy-blend dried yeast
2 tbsp caster (superfine) sugar
1 tsp fine sea salt
1 tbsp olive oil

1. Mix together the flours, yeast, sugar and salt. Stir the oil and 280ml of warm water into the dry ingredients. Knead the mixture on an oiled surface for 10 minutes.
2. Leave the dough to rest in a lightly oiled bowl, covered with oiled cling film, for 1–2 hours.
3. Knead for 2 more minutes then split it into 2 even pieces and shape into 2 round loaves. Transfer the cobs to a greased baking tray and cover with oiled cling film. Leave to prove for 1 hour.
4. Meanwhile, preheat the oven to 220°C (200°C fan) / 425F / gas 7.
5. Dust with flour and slash across the tops with a knife.
6. Transfer the tray to the oven then quickly throw a small cupful of water onto the oven floor and close the door.
7. Bake for 35–40 minutes or until the loaves sound hollow when you tap them underneath.

MAKES: **1** | PREP TIME: **2 HOURS 30 MINS** | COOKING TIME: **35-40 MINS**

Tuscan Saltless Bread

400 g / 14 oz / 2 ⅔ cups strong white bread flour, plus extra for dusting

½ tsp easy-blend dried yeast

2 tbsp olive oil

300 ml / 10 ½ fl. oz / 1 ⅓ cup warm water

1. Mix together the flour and yeast. Stir the oil into 280ml of warm water then stir it into the dry ingredients.

2. Knead the mixture on a lightly oiled surface with your hands for 10 minutes or until smooth and elastic.

3. Leave the dough to rest in a lightly oiled bowl, covered with oiled cling film, for 1–2 hours or until doubled in size.

4. Knead it for 2 more minutes, then shape into a round loaf.

5. Transfer the loaf to a greased baking tray and cover with oiled cling film. Leave to prove for 1 hour or until doubled in size.

6. Meanwhile, preheat the oven to 220°C (200°C fan) / 425F / gas 7.

7. Dust the loaf with flour and slash the top with a knife.

8. Transfer the tray to the top shelf of the oven then quickly throw a small cupful of water onto the oven floor and close the door.

9. Bake for 35–40 minutes or until the loaf sounds hollow when you tap it underneath.

10. Transfer to a wire rack and leave to cool.

MAKES: **2** | PREP TIME: **2 HOURS 30 MINS** | COOKING TIME: **35-40 MINS**

White Cob Loaf

400 g / 14 oz / 2 ⅔ cups strong white
bread flour, plus extra for dusting
½ tsp easy-blend dried yeast
1 tbsp caster (superfine) sugar
1 tsp fine sea salt
1 tbsp olive oil

1. Mix together the flour, yeast, sugar
   and salt. Stir the oil into 280ml of
   warm water then stir it into the dry
   ingredients.
2. Knead the mixture on a lightly
   oiled surface with your hands for
   10 minutes or until smooth
   and elastic.
3. Leave the dough to rest in a lightly
   oiled bowl, covered with oiled
   cling film, for 1–2 hours or until
   doubled in size.
4. Knead it for 2 more minutes then
   split it into 2 even pieces and
   shape into 2 round loaves.
5. Transfer the cobs to a greased
   baking tray and cover with oiled
   cling film. Leave to prove for
   1 hour or until doubled in size.
6. Meanwhile, preheat the oven to
   220°C (200°C fan) / 425F / gas 7.
7. Dust the cobs with flour and slash
   a cross in the tops with a knife.
8. Transfer the tray to the top shelf of
   the oven then quickly throw a
   small cupful of water onto the
   oven floor and close the door.
9. Bake for 35–40 minutes or until
   the loaves sound hollow when you
   tap them underneath.
10. Transfer to a wire rack and leave
    to cool.

MAKES: **1** | PREP TIME: **2 HOURS 30 MINS** | COOKING TIME: **35-40 MINS**

Garlic Mushroom Bread

200 g / 7 oz / 1 ⅓ cups strong white
    bread flour
200 g / 7 oz / 1 ⅓ cups rye flour
1 tsp easy-blend dried yeast
1 tbsp caster (superfine) sugar
1 tsp fine sea salt
1 tbsp olive oil

FOR THE MUSHROOMS
50 g / 1 ¾ oz / ¼ cup butter
300 g / 10 ½ oz chestnut mushrooms,
    sliced
2 cloves of garlic, crushed
50 g / 1 ¾ oz flat leaf parsley, chopped

1. Mix together the flours, yeast, sugar and salt. Stir the oil into 280ml of warm
   water and mix with the dry ingredients.
2. Knead the dough on a lightly oiled surface for 10 minutes or until smooth
   and elastic.
3. Leave the dough to rest, covered with oiled cling film, for 1–2 hours or until
   doubled in size.
4. Melt the butter in a sauté pan and add the mushrooms and plenty of salt and
   pepper. Cook for 10 minutes or until any liquid that comes out has
   evaporated. Add the garlic and parsley and cook for 2 minutes. Leave to cool.
5. Knead the mushrooms into the dough and shape into a square loaf.
6. Transfer it to a greased baking tray, cover with oiled cling film and prove until
   doubled in size.
7. Preheat the oven to 220°C (200°C fan) / 425F / gas 7.
8. Transfer the tray to the top shelf of the oven then quickly throw a small cupful
   of water onto the floor of the oven and close the door.
9. Bake for 35–40 minutes or until the loaf sounds hollow when tapped
   underneath. Transfer the bread to a wire rack and leave to cool.

Cheese and Herb Loaf

300 g / 10 ½ oz / 2 cup self-raising flour
2 tsp baking powder
250 g / 9 oz / 1 ¼ cup butter, softened
5 large eggs
100 g / 3 ½ oz / 1 cup Cheddar, grated
2 tbsp flat leaf parsley, chopped
2 tbsp chives, chopped

1. Preheat the oven to 170°C (150°C fan) / 340F / gas 3 and line a large loaf tin with non-stick baking paper.
2. Sieve the flour and baking powder into a mixing bowl and add the butter and eggs.
3. Beat the mixture with an electric whisk for 4 minutes or until smooth and well whipped.
4. Fold in the cheese and herbs then scrape the mixture into the loaf tin.
5. Bake for 55 minutes or until a skewer inserted in the centre comes out clean.
6. Transfer the cake to a wire rack and leave to cool completely before serving.

Parmesan and Olive Shortbread Biscuits

150 g / 5 oz / ⅔ cup butter, cubed
230 g / 8 oz / 1 ½ cup plain
  (all-purpose) flour
50 g / 1 ¾ oz / ½ cup Parmesan, grated
50 g / 1 ¾ oz / ⅓ cup black olives,
  pitted and finely chopped
sea salt flakes for sprinkling

1. Preheat the oven to 180°C (160°C fan) / 350F / gas 4 and line a baking tray with greaseproof paper.
2. Rub the butter into the flour and stir in the Parmesan and olives.
3. Knead gently until the mixture forms a smooth dough then form into a cylinder 6 cm in diameter.
4. Slice the roll into 1 cm thick slices and spread them out on the baking tray.
5. Bake the biscuits for 15–20 minutes, turning the tray round halfway through.
6. Sprinkle the biscuits with sea salt flakes then transfer to a wire rack and leave to cool.

SERVES: 6 | **PREP TIME: 2 HOURS 30 MINS** | **COOKING TIME: 25-35 MINS**

Sesame and Poppy Seed Focaccia

300 g / 10 ½ oz / 2 cups strong white bread flour
½ tsp easy-blend dried yeast
1 tsp fine sea salt
2 tbsp olive oil

TO FINISH
50 ml / 1 ¾ fl. oz / ¼ cup olive oil
50 ml / 1 ¾ fl. oz / ¼ cup warm water
½ tsp fine sea salt
1 tbsp sesame seeds
1 tbsp poppy seeds

1. Mix together the flour, yeast and salt. Stir in the oil and 280ml of warm water.
2. Knead the mixture on a lightly oiled surface for 10 minutes or until smooth and elastic.
3. Leave the dough to rest, covered with oiled cling film, for 1–2 hours or until doubled in size.
4. Oil a rectangular cake tin then stretch out the dough to cover the base.
5. Cover the focaccia with oiled cling film and leave to prove for 1 hour or until doubled in size.
6. Preheat the oven to 220°C (200°C fan) / 425F / gas 7.
7. Put the oil, water and salt in a jar and shake well.
8. Pour it all over the dough then sprinkle with the seeds.
9. Bake for 25–35 minutes or until the top is golden and the base is cooked through.
10. Leave to cool on a wire rack before cutting into squares.

MAKES: **4** | PREP TIME: **2 HOURS 30 MINS** | COOKING TIME: **25-30 MINS**

Wholemeal Sesame Baguettes

300 g / 10 ½ oz / 2 cup stoneground wholemeal flour

100 g / 3 ½ oz / ½ cup strong white bread flour, plus extra for dusting

½ tsp easy-blend dried yeast

2 tbsp caster (superfine) sugar

1 tsp fine sea salt

1 tbsp sesame oil

1 egg, beaten

3 tbsp sesame seeds

1. Mix together the flours, yeast, sugar and salt. Stir the oil and 280ml of warm water into the dry ingredients.

2. Knead the mixture on a lightly oiled surface with your hands for 10 minutes or until smooth and elastic.

3. Leave the dough to rest in an oiled bowl, covered with oiled film, for 2 hours. Knead it for 2 more minutes then split it into 4 even pieces and shape into baguettes.

4. Transfer the baguettes to a greased baking tray and cover with oiled cling film. Leave to prove for 1 hour.

5. Preheat the oven to 220°C (200°C fan) / 425F / gas 7.

6. Brush the baguettes with beaten egg and sprinkle with sesame seeds then slash across the tops with a knife.

7. Transfer the tray to the top shelf of the oven then quickly throw a small cupful of water onto the oven floor and close the door.

8. Bake for 25–30 minutes or until the loaves sound hollow when you tap them underneath.

MAKES: **1** | PREP TIME: **2 HOURS 30 MINS** | COOKING TIME: **35–40 MINS**

Spelt Bread

200 g / 7 oz / 1 ⅓ cup strong white bread flour, plus extra for dusting
200 g / 7 oz / 1 ⅓ cup spelt flour
½ tsp easy-blend dried yeast
1 tbsp caster (superfine) sugar
1 tsp fine sea salt
1 tbsp olive oil

1. Mix together the flours, yeast, sugar and salt. Stir in the oil and 280ml of warm water.
2. Knead on a lightly oiled surface for 10 minutes or until the dough is elastic.
3. Leave the dough to rest, covered with oiled cling film, for 1–2 hours or until doubled in size.
4. Knead the dough for 2 more minutes, then shape it into a round loaf.
5. Transfer the loaf to a greased baking tray and cover again with oiled cling film. Leave to prove for 1 hour or until doubled in size.
6. Preheat the oven to 220°C (200°C fan) / 430F / gas 7.
7. When the dough has risen, score the top with a knife and dust with flour.
8. Bake for 35–40 minutes. Transfer the bread to a wire rack and leave to cool.

MAKES: **1** | PREP TIME: **2 HOURS 30 MINS** | COOKING TIME: **50-55 MINS**

Onion Bread

2 large onions, peeled, quartered and sliced
3 tbsp olive oil
300 g / 10 ½ oz / 2 cup strong white bread flour, plus extra for dusting
100 g / 3 ½ oz / ⅔ cup stoneground wholemeal flour
½ tsp easy-blend dried yeast
1 tbsp caster (superfine) sugar
1 tsp fine sea salt
2 tbsp black onion seeds

1. Fry the onions in the oil for 15 minutes or until starting to caramelise.
   Leave to cool.
2. Mix together the flours, yeast, sugar and salt. Stir the onions and onion seeds
   into 280ml of warm water and stir into the dry ingredients.
3. Knead the mixture on a lightly oiled surface for 10 minutes or until the dough
   is smooth and elastic.
4. Leave the dough to rest in a lightly oiled bowl, covered with oiled cling film,
   for 1–2 hours.
5. Roll the dough into a fat sausage. Turn it 90°C and roll it tightly the other way
   then tuck the ends under and transfer the dough to a lined loaf tin, keeping
   the seam underneath.
6. Cover the tin with oiled cling film and leave for 1 hour.
7. Preheat the oven to 220°C (200°C fan) / 425F / gas 7.
8. Bake the loaf for 35–40 minutes or until the underneath sounds hollow
   when tapped.

MAKES: **12** | PREP TIME: **2 HOURS 30 MINS** | COOKING TIME: **15-20 MINS**

Parmesan Rolls

400 g / 14 oz / 2 ⅔ cup strong white
  bread flour
½ tsp easy-blend dried yeast
1 tbsp caster (superfine) sugar
1 tsp fine sea salt
1 tbsp olive oil
100 g / 3 ½ oz / 1 cup Parmesan,
  finely grated

1. In a large bowl, mix together the
   flour, yeast, sugar and salt. Stir in
   the oil, Parmesan and 280ml of
   warm water.
2. Knead the mixture on a lightly
   oiled surface with your hands for
   10 minutes or until smooth
   and elastic.
3. Leave the dough to rest in a lightly
   oiled bowl, covered with oiled cling
   film, for 1–2 hours.
4. Knead it for 2 more minutes then
   split it into 12 even pieces and
   shape into rolls.
5. Transfer the rolls to a greased
   baking tray and cover with oiled
   cling film. Leave to prove for
   1 hour.
6. Preheat the oven to
   220°C (200°C fan) / 425F/ gas 7.
7. Cut a cross in the top of each roll
   and transfer the tray to the top
   shelf of the oven.
8. Bake for 15–20 minutes or until
   the rolls sound hollow when you
   tap them underneath.
9. Transfer to a wire rack and leave
   to cool.

Index